The Woman Who Wouldn't Quit

Unbreakable Spirit

by *Paula Aldis*

The Woman Who Wouldn't Quit

Unbreakable Spirit

by *Paula Aldis*

ROSALES MAVERICKS PUBLISHING STUDIO

New York | Las Vegas | Guadalajara

Title: The Woman Who Wouldn't Quit
Subtitle: Unbreakable Spirit

ISBN: 978-1-969745-07-2 (English Paperback)
ISBN: 978-1-959471-99-8 (English Hardback)
ISBN: 978-1-959471-98-1 (English eBook)

Library of Congress Control Number: 2025927154

Categories: Memoir / Military Life / Autobiography

Cover design by: RMPStudio™
Interior design: RMPStudio™ Team
Photography Cover Image: Kari Aldis
Editor: RMPStudio™ Editorial Division

ORDERING INFORMATION: https://www.adriana.company/authorpaulaaldis
This work is a memoir based on the author's personal experiences and recollections. Certain names, places, and events may have changed for privacy or narrative purposes. While every effort has been made to ensure accuracy, the author and publisher make no representations or warranties regarding the completeness or accuracy of the content and disclaim all liability for any loss or damage arising from its use. This book hit #1 Hot New Release on Amazon on 11/17/2025 and Top #3 Bestseller on 11/23/2025 at 4:23pm Pacific.

Printed in Las Vegas, Nevada, United States of America
Manufactured in the United States of America

Rosales Mavericks Publishing Studio™| 1180 N. Town Center Dr., Suite 100 Las Vegas, Nevada 89144 | www.Adriana.Company |Office 201.500.5902

Quote:

"The scars will always be there, but I now see these scars as reminders of what I have been through. I wear them like my tattoos. I wear them with pride."

~Paula Aldis

Dedications

I am dedicating this book first to my mother. I appreciated all the times she had to step up and care for me. Thank You, Mom. I love and miss you dearly.

I want to thank my family, friends, endorsers, doctors, and my therapists, my power people, for always being there for me when I needed it most.

I want to give a great, big thanks to my sister Jennifer. You stepped up and came and took excellent care of our mom, and now you are living with our dad. You have gone above and beyond, Girl! I Love You!

I want to thank my beautiful, loving, caring, and amazing children. You two have made my life complete, and you are my purpose in this life. I adore you, Tyler, and Kari. I love you!!!!!

My biggest thank you to my husband, Chris. You have put up with so much from me over the past 35 years. Thanks for working on us with me and never giving up. I love you tremendously and always will!

Adriana Rosales, my publisher. This was quite the journey for the two of us. We have become good friends during this process and have discovered that we share several parallels in our lives. Your RMPStudio™ is amazing, and you all have put so much work into me and my dream. Thank you for all your dedication to me and my story.

Table of Contents

Foreword

There are moments in life when a story arrives not simply to be read but to be felt, deeply, profoundly, and personally. The Woman Who Wouldn't Quit: Unbreakable Spirit is one of those stories.

From the very first page, Paula Aldis draws us into the sacred territory where pain and purpose meet. Her journey, illuminated by faith and anchored in love, reminds us that even in the darkest hours, the light of grace can guide us home. This is not merely a story about survival; it is a song of renewal.

As I turned each page, I was reminded of the many women I've met across continents who carry silent battles behind their brave smiles. Paula gives voice to that collective courage. Through the trials of Type 1 diabetes, near-death encounters, and the unrelenting tests of body and soul, she shows us that perseverance is not just endurance; it is a spiritual art form.

Her humor in hardship, her faith in fear, and her ability to rise again and again embody what I call the Authentic Harmony of the Human Spirit, where strength and surrender coexist. Paula's unbreakable will does not roar with defiance; it whispers with grace. It teaches us that healing begins not when the pain ends, but when the heart chooses to love in spite of it.

In every chapter, Paula stands as a lighthouse for others navigating turbulent seas. She proves that miracles often bloom in the soil of adversity, and that the most significant victories are those born of unwavering faith and compassion.

To read this book is to be reminded of our shared humanity, the truth that we are all designed to rise, to heal, and to shine. Paula's story is a testament to the divine resilience that lives within us all.

May her journey inspire you to keep walking your own, with courage, laughter, and an unbreakable spirit that refuses to quit.

With heartfelt admiration and infinite light,

Dr. Pauline Crawford, Author - The Power of Authentic Harmony, Founder, Corporate Heart International, Vice President, International University of Entreprenology, President, World Association of Visioners & Entreprenologists

Introduction

My name is Paula Aldis, and I am writing my memoir to help others understand who I am. By reading my book, you will get a true sense of what I have been through. The hardships, struggles, and triumphs were what made me who I am today. I have often been told that I am here for a reason and that I have a purpose. Maybe I just haven't found that reason or my purpose yet. I hope writing about my life's journey and sharing the truth behind it will help make my purpose clear. My journey has been long and difficult. I'm ready to venture back in time and re-live this journey once more, putting it behind me and moving on to the next chapter of my life. Our lives are full of struggles and triumphs. How we weather these struggles depends on how we prepare for what is next.

Readers will see that nothing in life is a given. Giving up is not a choice! Even the most difficult struggles will eventually come to an end, and your life will continue. I did just that, and hopefully so can you. So, whenever you feel like giving up, look again!

Receiving the life-altering diagnosis of Type 1 diabetes at the tender age of twelve is when my real life's journey began, and all the hardships I would face became my new way of life. You will read about the difficulties with my disease, other diagnoses I received, the medical malpractice I have endured, and the issues with my family. It has been a challenging, but beautiful life for me, and I am still here to get it out and let it all go. I often wonder what else I can take if life could possibly get any harder. You will read all this in my story, and you will also gain insight into the strength I have found within myself.

"You have a purpose." I hope that by writing my memoir, I will discover my purpose in life, and that purpose will help others find theirs and never give up on themselves. Perhaps my purpose is to serve as an example of perseverance and to always find triumphs.

So, I say to you, find your own triumphs!

Chapter 1: Before Diagnosis

I grew up in an incredibly happy home, and I was one of six children in a military family. My early years were amazing. I have had the opportunity to experience living in many different places. I was born in Maine. We then moved to Michigan, then off to New Hampshire, and then, after that tour, we were off to Arkansas. However, the best place I can say was my father's next tour, Hawaii. This was the one place we lived the longest. This was a five-year tour for Dad and our family. This is also where my baby sister was born.

Living in a big family was full of adventures. With all the moving around and new states, we were given such incredible opportunities and experiences. Getting a layout of the states and seeing what these places had to offer our family was our parents' goal. I lived in Maine, Michigan, New Hampshire, Arkansas, and now Hawaii. I even spent time in Massachusetts and Kansas, where our grandparents used to live. My mother was from Kansas, and my father was from Massachusetts. They met when my father got stationed in my mother's hometown, Salina, Kansas. They married here and were off to Alaska. I was made in Alaska, before my father's next set of orders, which took us to my birthplace, Maine. Each state we lived in made a mark on my life. Some more than others. Our time in Blytheville, Arkansas was a challenging time for us all. We were "base kids." This town we lived in was an incredibly old southern town with a small Air Force base. Our family faced a lot of prejudice. My father is very dark-skinned, and so are some of us kids. We were considered outsiders. We experienced corporal punishment in schools. When I got out of my seat to sharpen a pencil without permission from my teacher, I got my hands hit with a ruler to teach me a lesson. It felt like we were their targets. We weren't there long, and my father put in for new orders. We were not happy living there, so off again we went.

My younger sister, just over a year younger, was my best friend. Our mother always dressed us up in matching outfits. She made almost every outfit for us. Her sewing talents were amazing. She was extremely crafty. I guess that's where I got my crafting skills. My sister and I used to dress alike until we started school. We were inseparable, and even shared friends. We were very mischievous rugrats, but always happy and found fun in everything we did. We even got in trouble together.

The adventures continued, and we were now off to a new state. The state of Hawaii. We were all extremely excited to go to Hawaii, but not too sure about what was in store for us there. These were some of the best times of my life. Every weekend was spent hours upon hours at the beach. I'm talking about all-day trips. We would meet up with the families of our parents, kids, and all. The food was amazing. My dad would spend all night preparing the teriyaki meals, and my mom would make her famous coleslaw, potato salad, amazing desserts, and my favorite potato packets. It was just wonderful. The fun, food, and friends. From daylight to nightfall.

We were all at the age when we enjoyed playing sports, and having five kids in different sports must have been hard for my parents. I was extremely interested in playing softball and became particularly good at it. I had siblings in basketball, football, baseball, and, of course, softball. Even my parents played on intramural softball teams. We all got our athletic abilities from Dad. He was always involved in the base sports programs. He was my first coach ever.

These were the times in my life when I truly experienced what it was like to have friends. Moving every three years, sometimes often, made it difficult to maintain steady friendships. We moved to Hawaii when I was in second grade, which was when I was seven years old. We lived in base housing on Hickam AFB. There were so many kids for us to become friends with. Several families had kids of the same ages. Having many children was a common occurrence back in those days. We spent our weekends camping out in the backyard, with the boys on one side of the yard and the girls on the other. We spent hours upon hours climbing trees and setting up tree swings. It didn't matter if it was light or dark out; we were climbing that banyan tree in the backyard. Climbing the barbed-wire fence to school every morning and back over after school let out was also something we did. The Nuns got a kick out of it. There was an awful lot of climbing back in those days.

We built our own golf course in the backyard. We would play silly things like roller derby, crack the whip, and all the other childhood games, only at a higher level. One neighbor's father worked on the flight line and had two giant inner tube tires. We would take those tubes with us to the beach and ride the waves. We stacked them on top of each other, and we would pile on top.

The first person to fall off lost. This did not always end well. My sister was the loser, being the first to fall off and fracturing her arm. There were several injuries among us, including me. I fell out of the banyan tree when the rope swing broke. I came down hard and suffered a hip injury. My father was in Korea when this happened, so our neighbor came out to pick me up. He saw the whole thing happen. He was a tiny man, but he found the strength to pick me up and carry me into the house. I was brought to the base clinic, but there were no broken bones, just a lot of pain.

I still got up the next morning and walked to school. The fun continued. There would be days when we would spend the entire day at the base pools. We would go on all-day bike excursions. It was safe back in those days, especially for us base kids, and we would take the city bus to Waikiki beach and crash the hotel pools. It was a funny sight to see, sometimes ten or more kids getting off the city bus and just running free. These times were very memorable for me. It was also great to have friends for longer than three years. Life was good there, not just for me, but for my whole family.

Towards the end of my father's tour in Hawaii, we welcomed my younger sister to the family. I was nine years old when she was born. We had two more years left in Hawaii. The last year we spent in Hawaii was very rough for my mom. My father got orders to Korea for an entire year. There she was, a new mother of her sixth child, as all her children participated in sports and numerous school functions, which often led to injuries and illnesses. She did it all on her own with very little money. Additionally, living in Hawaii can mean being away from family on the mainland. We occasionally had people visit, but that wasn't often. After my sister's birth, my father's mother came from Boston to help my mom and spent a couple of weeks with us. My mother's parents came from Kansas for a month during the holidays. They also helped my mother financially. I'm not sure how much of a break it was for her, though. She made it work. I never gave my mom the credit or the respect she deserved for being our mother. I now understand how difficult that must have been for her, and I respect her even more.

Upon my father's return to the island, he informed us that we would be moving to Albuquerque, New Mexico, on a base called Kirtland AFB, from beach life to the desert. This news was very hard for all of us. It was the longest we had ever lived in one place. We truly got a sense of what it was like to have long-time friends. We all loved the beach life and the constant warm weather. So, here we go again. Pack the household goods and say our goodbyes. This is the rinse-and-repeat cycle for this military family. It became much harder with age as well.

There was something else going on with me at this time. Something was off. I wasn't feeling energetic or happy. I noticed I was losing weight and had a constant thirst that I just couldn't quench. I was also using the restroom more than usual. I would have to ask for permission in almost every class to be excused. I would get up several times a night. This was my body trying to tell me something, what was it? I thought, "What's wrong with me?"

I kept it to myself, though. I thought my parents would be mad at me, so I kept quiet. My mother had bought a new traveling outfit for me to wear for our long plane flight. When I tried the pants on, they were a little snug when she first gave them to me. On the day of our flight to leave Hawaii, I noticed the pants had become loose and didn't fit the same. I wondered if anyone else had noticed, but no one mentioned it to me.

Time to load onto the plane and say our final goodbyes. I remember me and my sister's best friends, and their families had come to say goodbye. My brother's good friends also showed up. The gate area was full of our family and friends. There were plenty of tears that day. Aloha Hawaii!

Chapter 2: The Diagnosis

My childhood was amazing, and I was happy. I wasn't prepared for what was in store for me and my near future. We arrived in New Mexico. I had just finished sixth grade and was twelve years old in 1977. We again moved into base housing and managed to make friends right away. But I wasn't feeling like myself at all. Trying my hardest to act like all was fine with me. Still not feeling my best, I got on a softball team, and thankfully, my new friends were all on the team. My father took over the coaching position and again was going to be my softball coach. He always made sure we stayed active and got involved in team sports. Prior to my season starting, I just didn't have that energetic feeling anymore. Something just wasn't right with me.

The family settled into Albuquerque pretty quickly. We were used to doing this. I started in seventh grade. Not even one month after starting this new school, I became very ill. I had what seemed to my parents and me to be a type of flu. In and out of school. Going for one week and then missing the following week. I became extremely thin. After this went on for several weeks, my parents finally decided to take me to the base acute care clinic to find out what was going on with me. On this day, I had my blood drawn. That was a first for me. I passed out after seeing the needle, then I saw the blood being withdrawn. All that blood! This frightened me. I had never experienced anything like that before. After several hours in the clinic, the doctor returned and informed my father and me that I had epilepsy. I knew what that was. There was a boy in my PE class who had it and had to wear a helmet. I remember seeing several of his seizures. Was I going to have to wear a helmet whenever I wanted to play? What about softball? Would I be able to play my favorite sport? This was very confusing for me and my father. There were no incidents of me ever suffering from any type of seizure. I left more confused than when we first arrived. Could this really be what's wrong with me?

My parents received a call later that day from the doctor who had seen me earlier. He gave them the news that I had Juvenile Diabetes, and they needed to have me admitted to the hospital the next day. My parents both had relatives who had diabetes, but they were adults, and all they knew was that they had to take something called insulin. I was admitted to BCMC, the Bernalillo County Medical Center, in the heart of Albuquerque, NM. This is where it all began for me.

My journey in life had been sidetracked. It was terrifying for me. The hospital was large and filled with other sick children. Some of them looked severely sick, too. I was informed I would be there for at least one week. I had never even been in a hospital before. The atmosphere was somber, and it didn't seem like I would enjoy my stay. After the shock and realization of where I was sunk in, I unpacked my bag and put on my pajamas. I then got into my bed and looked over at this young girl in the bed next to me. I'd spend my days and nights with her. Would I even like her? She was a little older than I was. It was revealed to me and my parents that she had Juvenile Rheumatoid Arthritis. It was clear she was in a lot of pain. My parents remained with me for a while, a few hours, and on their way out, my roommate's family came in for a visit. They introduced themselves to one another, and I noticed her brother. He looked familiar to me when I realized he was in a couple of my classes at Middle School. I felt a little better about being there, and we connected because of her brother. My parents said their goodbyes, and I again felt so alone. What now? What was next for me and this journey I was now on?

A doctor and several nurses entered our room not long after my parents left. One of the nurses was holding an orange and what looked to me like the stuff for taking more blood. Not again, I thought. I absolutely knew nothing about Juvenile Diabetes. My doctor tried his hardest to explain my diagnosis and what it meant for me. I was so dazed and confused by what he was throwing at me. Did I just hear him say that I would have to live the rest of my life by taking medicine through a needle? I was told that this is the only treatment for my new disease. I wished my parents were still there with me. He excused himself and left, and I soon learned what the orange and needles were for.

My first lesson was about to begin. I was shown how to withdraw something called insulin into a syringe, still in major shock. How could this be what I'm experiencing in my life, and at this age? The orange was brought out next in my lesson. I was shown how to inject the orange with this insulin stuff. The orange signified my leg or my lower stomach. It signified the fat I would squeeze to inject insulin from the syringe into myself. We repeated this process, and upon the nurse's departure, she informed me that she would be back later that day with more lessons. She would be showing me how to check my urine for sugar and ketones. This was done in little glass beakers with large tablets. My levels were extremely high, of course. This scared me even more because I was informed that high sugar levels were not a good thing with diabetics. My numbers were in the 500s. This meant my disease was not in control, and I had been living like this for quite a long time. I was also informed I would have to repeat this process, collecting my pee, using a tear dropper to transport the right amount into the glass beaker, dropping the tablets, one at a time, into the pee, and checking the results on a color chart. I would be doing this upon waking up, before every meal, and prior to going to bed, also I would be woken up at 3:00 am. That was the hardest because I just wanted to stay in bed. My thoughts became very negative. How was I going to do this every day and night, and for the rest of my life?

The day was moving along, and it had now gotten close to dinner time. A dietitian came into my room and handed me a menu to look over. I was told I could only have 1,200 calories a day, with no sugar. This was a bummer. I loved my sweets. Wait, was that why I became diabetic? After my diet plan for my stay was completed, the dietician let me know that my disease was something called an autoimmune condition. It wasn't my fault! The amount of sugar I had consumed had nothing to do with me getting this disease, but now it would determine how I would survive with this disease. My nurse soon left my room, returned, and handed me some insulin vials, a syringe, and said it was time to recheck my urine, and then I would give myself my first injection. Was I going to be able to do this? I started crying and shaking so badly. The nurse did give me some encouragement, and I settled down and did an okay job. I did leave a bruise at the injection site, though. The nurse informed me that that could happen from time to time. She told me I had probably hit a blood vessel. That left a large bump that hurt to touch. This was a regular occurrence for me at first. My nurse showed me some tricks to avoid this from happening. I started feeling better about what I was facing, but it was still quite the shock and a shock that would take me a very long time to truly get past.

The rest of my stay at BCMC was full of lessons about Diabetes and what my diagnosis meant for me. I was told that I would not be able to have children. It could cause me to have kidney failure and shorten my life. I was told that diabetics are prone to having amputations, blindness, kidney disease, and heart disease. I was told that my life span would be shorter than that of my peers. All this was so much to take in, especially for a twelve-year-old with no one with her to help her take it all in. I was feeling so alone in this. I was so young, but I couldn't tell my family, especially my parents, how I really felt. I actually felt this was my doom!

Chapter 3: The Early Years

My first year as a diabetic was a big learning experience for me and my family. Learning about the importance of insulin, diet control, exercise, and keeping my sugars at a certain level. I did not have a grasp on my new diet restriction, though. I was only twelve and turned thirteen during this time. I just didn't realize that even though I felt healthy, I really wasn't. Just because there was a diagnosis, I was now aware that this was going to be a lifelong struggle for me. I had to grow up fast! My family was clueless as to caring for a young diabetic, as well. We had to learn all of this together. They saw me acting and feeling fine. I never felt sick after eating the forbidden foods, so I thought I was doing fine. No one else saw me feeling off, so there were no questions about how I was doing with my disease. I wasn't checking my urine as I was told to. I would fudge my results. Who would ever question it? But I soon found out how wrong I was with what I was and was not doing. Almost a year after my diagnosis, I experienced my first episode of what is called DKA, Diabetes Ketoacidosis. This was a new one for me. My blood sugars got into a dangerous range, and my body started becoming extremely acidic. This was a violent illness. I sometimes compare it to chemo sickness. A lot of burning vomiting, and every inch of my body hurts. This episode happened while I was at a sleepover at my best friend's house next door. My friend's mother carried me back home, and my mother took me to the hospital right away. This was when I learned about that part of my disease. Like I said, this disease was a learning experience for me, and this was a lesson I wish I had never learned. At least not in that way.

Recovery came quickly for me. I found it very strange that there was no one that I was aware of having the same disease as me. Was I alone? Apparently not. That day had finally come, but was I ready for it? In my third year with diabetes, I was invited to my sister's boyfriend's house. He had a sister my age, and I would play with her while my sister hung out with her boyfriend. I'm sure to make out. His sister and I went into her neighborhood to play with some of the other kids. This was when I met the first kid with diabetes. Actually, I didn't meet him; I was just told he too had juvenile diabetes. Another like me, I thought. It was a scary experience for me. He was completely bald, and I was told by her that it was a complication of his diabetes. She thought it was funny. Did this mean I would lose my hair, like him? I lived with that fear for a long time. I couldn't get that boy out of my mind. No, it couldn't be, not my hair!

I loved living in New Mexico. I had many friends, started High School, and played softball on the Junior Varsity team. I loved being by the mountains and all the adventures we experienced. We spent a lot of time in the mountains hiking, even tubing on the snow-covered mountains each winter. New Mexico is full of very historic and Native American towns. We went to several of these cities. My favorite was Santa Fe. I was always trying my hardest to keep up with all my peers. Hiding my disease was getting easier for me. I never talked or complained about my disease. This was also the place where I experienced going out on dates. I even double-dated with my older sister.

My father retired from the Air Force during our last year in New Mexico. After attending a trade school there It was our last year there when he accepted a job in the state of Virginia. We were on the move again. I was fifteen, going to be sixteen years of age; the year was 1980, and it was starting all over again. That was quite a trip. My mother did all the driving with four kids and our dog, Poochie. First, from New Mexico, we headed to Kansas to pick up Grandpa. After loading all the extras from our grandparents' house, we were on the road again. The car, an Oldsmobile, a white station wagon with wood side panels, was stuffed full of five suitcases on the roof. We had a lot of fun moments on that trip. The funniest thing was when Grandpa put his hat on, which meant his Milk of Magnesia was kicking in, and my mom had to pull over quickly. My brother would always run and get into the bathroom first, and Grandpa would be dancing around, about to lose it. So, off we headed to a new state, a new high school, new friends, and learned another local culture. This trip was a new way for me, though. I started this transition as a diabetic.

I still was not as disciplined with my disease as I should have been. I just wanted to be like the other high schoolers, and I didn't want anyone to know what I truly was. A Diabetic who had to check her urine and take shots daily. There were also the dietary restrictions I had to constantly be aware of. I did meet a great friend my first year in VA. We became very close and spent a lot of time at each other's houses. I attended all her cross-country meets, and we attended our first concert together. But she soon moved back to Mississippi with her adoptive mother. This was hard for me at the time. She understood my diabetes and didn't treat me any differently because of it: finally, someone who understood me for me and my condition.

This was not my first year of high school. I decided I would try out for the softball team. I was a pretty talented player, but I got cut. This left me with one other option: I joined the city recreation softball league. I played on this team for three years. I suffered from one episode of DKA during these three years of high school. I wasn't aware of any other students or team members with diabetes. This was something I wanted in my life. I needed someone like me, someone who would understand what I was going through in my everyday life. I couldn't wait to get out of high school and broaden my horizons.

College was next for me. I attended the local community college. I was working on my associate's degree in business finance. I worked at a department store called Bradlees. This was when I met the best group of friends. These girls were everything to me. They didn't care that I was diabetic and always watched out for me. I attended college with several members of our group and would meet up on campus with them often. I was finally getting comfortable sharing my diabetes story with others.

I was now 18 years old and entering my early adult years. My body was going through some major changes, and my disease was too. Let the learning about my disease continue.

Chapter 4: Early Adulthood

These years are supposed to be the best years of my life. The most memorable years for me. I was so excited to be at this age. I just didn't know what that meant for my disease. As I mentioned previously, living with my diagnosis of juvenile diabetes, which was now called Type 1 Diabetes, was a learning experience. I learned that a diabetic's immune system is weak, and catching stuff going around is a given.

As I was getting along in my first year of college, and doing very well, I had caught Mononucleosis, or Mono for short. I don't know who I caught it from, when, or where. Not one of my friends had it. Maybe I caught it from someone who may have brushed up against me, or I sat in a seat that was contaminated. The weight started coming off fast. I lost over sixty pounds and was becoming extremely weak and tired. This diagnosis also made my immune system even weaker than it already was. I caught everything that was going around at work and at school. I was sick and tired of being sick and tired.

After recovering from mono, I was ready to get into the life of a college student again. I had a great friend group, and I was prepared to get up and out. Start experiencing the fun parts of college life. I started going out several nights a week and partied a little too much. My friends and I were aware of every party and had a club to go to most nights. This lifestyle took a toll on diabetic life. I was experiencing some episodes of DKA and became very unhealthy. I was having a great time, though. But this lifestyle started affecting every aspect of my life, especially my diabetes. I would get sick, and I was having to either drop classes or fail out. I was going nowhere, and I was going there fast. I needed to change, and I needed to do it quickly!

These were the days when I started dating. I was a mystery to many. I was tall, very thin, and I was an extremely quiet woman. I was hiding my disease as well. Guys didn't want to know this about me. There were nights I would go out with my friends and would not say a word. I just observed the other's behavior. This was all new to me. This one guy even asked me if I spoke English. The guys I dated were all fun. I went on dates to amusement parks, went skiing, and took many beach trips. I was starting to feel like I belonged, and this is going to be my own life now, and with my new friend group, forever.

Now it is time to tell you about my group of friends. We all grew up the same way. All had fathers in the military and retired to Virginia Beach. This group of girls had been best friends since elementary school, but they accepted me into their circle when we were all eighteen years old. I worked with my best friend and formed a friendship right away. She was so welcoming to me, and so were the rest of the girls. They really brought me out of my shell. The fun we had was immeasurable. On many occasions, after getting off work around eleven o'clock pm, we would load up one of our cars and head out of town for a road trip. We were constantly meeting new groups of people. We often ran into people we had already met while in another city. I never had a boring time with them; we always had fun. It was always such a memorable time. We often livened up some boring parties. I was having a blast at this time of my life.

I started taking better care of myself. Travel school was my next endeavor. I started this new adventure with such gusto. I was going to become a travel agent and start traveling all over the world. My grades were amazing, and I became the top student in our class. This was new for me. School never came easily for me; I was an average student for sure. I was excited and ready for what this venture was offering me. This was what I wanted for myself.

I loved where I was heading and enjoyed the process when, out of the blue, eating became very difficult for me. I started missing classes regularly. It became extreme. Every day it got worse. I was becoming very thin and malnourished. My mother took me to several doctors during this time. No one had an answer to what was going on with me and my health. I started experiencing severe low blood sugars with no explanation. I awoke in a hospital bed, not knowing how or when I got there, on several occasions. I was in horrible shape. It took eight months and three different hospitals to finally diagnose what was going on with me. At this time, my weight plummeted to 89 lbs., and I was now on over ten new medications. I had a diabetic condition called Gastroparesis. During this new, strange turn in my life, and my lack of ability to eat, I became severely malnourished and lost a lot of my bone density. My blood pressure would bottom out when I stood up, causing several fainting incidents. One of these incidents happened when I was in the hospital. I stood up, and my blood pressure dropped so dramatically that I passed out and ended up fracturing my femur in my right leg. That night, I was rushed into surgery and had a rod and screws placed to make repairs to the fractured bone. This is a lot for a twenty-two-year-old to manage. This was one of my first life-threatening experiences. Doctors had told me this would not end well for me. I could suffer a heart attack, and I could lose all organ functions. This brought back those early lessons with my initial diagnosis. Was my life going to end soon? The outcome looked bleak for me.

All I was waiting for was a reason and a treatment to end this horrible time. The doctors were at a loss. They felt it was best to put me on the Psychiatric ward of the hospital and treat me as a depressed anorexic. I was placed under the care of a very caring, smart, and brilliant Psychiatrist. He noticed right away that this was not a self-induced condition. That's when he worked with my Endocrinologist and came to the agreement to treat me with an IV form of a medication called Reglan. This worked wonderfully! I was able to treat this. I was getting better. This was what I needed to hear. I was getting close to my end.

What I had just gone through with having doctors tell me I wouldn't live past this, I felt I showed them how I was a true survivor. When I was in the middle of this, I convinced myself that I would never make it to forty, let alone live through this. I was ok with this and was at peace with it. I often prayed for God to take me away in my sleep.

This experience was extremely difficult for me. I got through the toughest of these days with the support and love of my family and, of course, my friend group. They came and visited me at the hospital and at our home. I had several family members, brothers, sisters, aunts and uncles, cousins, and my parents who were there for me during this time. They were able to give me some hope. I decided that when this was over, I was going to try to become a very healthy, proactive diabetic, and I would see my fortieth birthday.

My recovery was a long one. I was ready for what was next in my life journey. I was no longer able to continue in school, and I tried my hand at working. The jobs wouldn't last because of my poor health. I took this time to learn, on my own, all I could about Type 1 Diabetes and all the latest treatments. Constant blood checks were all new to me. No more urine testing. Oh, how times were changing for my disease and my life. I was accepted into The Diabetes Institute with several diabetes researchers. My diabetes came into tight control, and I found my way again.

There were still those thoughts I would have about ever meeting the right person and starting a family. I came with a full plate. Would I ever find a man willing to take all this on and include me in his life? Would this man be okay with not having children? Is he willing to have a short time with me? So many times, I thought "would this man be okay with my disease?" and having a life with me. Would my life ever be complete?

I started going out with my friends again. They even took me on a road trip right after one of my hospital stays. I felt full again, and I was glad God didn't answer my prayers for him to take me.

Chapter 5: The Right One

I was finally feeling a little bit of normalcy in my life again. My friends were there for me, and I was enjoying getting the chance to do things with them again. I have always loved throwing dinner parties. It was coming up on St. Patrick's Day. I was planning a traditional New England boiled dinner with corned beef, carrots, potatoes, and cabbage. I invited all my friends and their dates. I even had a setup date that night. My date was a Navy Pilot and an enormous Star Trek enthusiast, totally not my thing. One of the couples mentioned that her boyfriend's roommate was home that night and wasn't doing anything. I had them call him and invite him over. His name was Chris. He was a Hospital Corpsman, enlisted in the Navy. He was in his third year of the Navy. He was called and invited over. He was excited to come and meet new people.

My date was a big bore. When Chris arrived, I liked what I saw, and him. He returned the flirting as well. I made him the bartender for the evening, and he was happy to take the job on the spot. I even put a holiday garter around his arm for all the tips. We talked a lot in the kitchen. I learned about him, and he learned about me and my circumstances. Dinner went great! Chris and I sat next to each other. I think he was impressed with my cooking skills. So much fun, and the laughs didn't stop. The night was still young, so the decision was made to go to the club and dance. My date didn't dance, but Chris did. We danced several times that night and had a blast and a memorable evening.

There was no love connection with my date, but I was attracted to this Chris guy. After some working out amongst our friends, we were finally going on a lunch date. There was certainly an attraction there. The date was at a cute little beach spot, "The Raven."

We started dating after that day. The attraction was strong, and we always had a great time. Chris was leaving for North Carolina for some special training. He would come back to Virginia Beach on his weekends. I always had fun things planned for us. There was one trip I had planned for us and our friends to meet Chris in the OBX (Outer Banks), NC. It was an amazing weekend. We had so much fun together.

While Chris was in this training class, I decided to visit my sister in Arizona. We also went to California to visit our brother. While I was on this trip, I somehow fractured my left foot. It was either playing tennis or climbing the four stories at my sister's apartment complex. Who knows? I spent two days in a hospital in Arizona. The doctors were a little uneasy about my traveling on a plane with this fracture. I said, "Release me," and I got on that plane and returned home. I did just that and made it home fine. My foot was in a cast, and I waited for Chris to come back. Surprise, I broke my foot!

Upon Chris's return from training, he would be heading to Okinawa, Japan, for a one-year tour. We agreed that I would go to Detroit, Michigan, where he was from. Where his whole family was from and still lived. We got into his Cadillac, all packed up, and started our adventure to Detroit. We made one stop in South

Bend, Indiana. My older sister and her family lived there. It was a good stop for us. Chris met another one of my sisters. He still had several of my other siblings to meet. This would take him a while. My siblings all lived in different states. We left Indiana and headed north. It was a very long trip, and we were both ready for this trip to be over.

We pulled up to his childhood home. On the front porch there were so many people. Chris comes from a big family, too. I got out of Chris's large Cadillac with a cast on my left foot. This was in the heart of Detroit, and I certainly did not fit in.

They had a party planned for that night. I met so many people. I was overwhelmed! This was when his family and Chris got a true sense of me and my disease. The food was new to me, and I did not eat it. After the party was over and all the friends and family had gone home, we finally got to bed. Not even thinking of what was about to happen with the lack of food, my blood sugar dropped, and I went into one of my infamous low blood sugar incidents. Hypoglycemia. I awoke to his mother and Chris spooning juice into my mouth. The sheets were drenched with the sweat I had worked up. Welcome to Detroit!

I stayed in Detroit for the entire month. We went camping, went to a Detroit Tigers game, met more people, and even saw some inner-city drama out front of their family home. What an experience this trip was for me. It was time for me to head back home to Virginia Beach, and Chris would be heading to Japan for an entire year. We said our goodbyes, and I walked across the tarmac and got on the plane. There were plenty of thoughts going through my head for the whole trip home. Is this going to work out? How is this going to work? I had a hard time with this arrangement. I'm sure he did as well. But we were willing to make this work.

It had been two months into Chris's tour in Okinawa, and I received a letter from him. These were the days when writing letters was our only way of communication. It was expensive to make calls, so I would only call him once a month. This letter was a marriage proposal. It said, "This is not the traditional way of doing this, but would you marry me"? That's all it said. So, I replied with my one-word answer. YES! On a poster board, decorated with pictures and drawings. It was a little corny.

The proposal was made. The answer was given. Now what? I started shopping for dresses, shoes, and other wedding day things. I started planning the type of wedding we would have. Who I wanted included in the wedding party and all those wedding things. After the proposal, Chris's sister came and stayed with me at my parents' house. She was engaged, too. We were making plans to be involved in each other's weddings. This was so exciting for me. I was going to get married! I then went to a bridal show. There, I won a flower package for our wedding. My friends threw a bridal party for me at one of our favorite clubs and showered me with gifts.

I wasn't even married yet. That was a big question for me as well. When and where would we get married? Was I jumping the gun? The answers came in Chris's eighth month of his tour. He signed up for a training class to be held in California. He asked me to fly out to Reno, Nevada, and we could get married there. I guess I was about to elope. I did just that. I flew to Reno, and there was Chris, my brother, and his new wife at the airport. Surprise! I wasn't told about my brother. That was the first time Chris had met him. Thank God they were there for us. They also got the job of standing in as our witnesses. Chris had his best man, and I had my maid of honor. Bonus! My brother has such funny stories about their first meeting at the airport. He only knew Chris's first name. They called out his name. There he was, a young military guy, with a high and tight haircut. He was standing by the window, looking both nervous and eager. He wasn't what they had imagined. Chris greeted them with such warmth that my brother instantly knew he could trust him being with me. Chris spoke from his heart and told them, with no hesitation, that "Paula" was the love of his life. Right then and there, they knew that this was real.

Chris and I did not have much money, and this was going to be a week-long trip. My brother helped with our hotel and took us to see a show. My brother was just happy to be gambling. They planned to drive us up to Lake Tahoe, CA. They were planning to go skiing after our wedding.

We arrived at Lake Tahoe, and a blizzard started while we were on our way up. It was a scary trip. We had to pull over and put chains on the tires. People were getting turned around because they didn't have chains. This gave Chris and my brother some bonding time. My brother and his wife were excited about the amount of snow falling. We found a cute little chapel, and we were ready. Or were we? We both had those thoughts, are we doing the right thing? My brother always says my father told him not to screw this up! Several feet of snow fell that night, but we managed and had our reception at Carlos Murphy's, a Mexican restaurant. It was such a fun night. At the restaurant, our waiter made us some funny-looking balloon hats. We wore those silly hats for the rest of the evening. We did it!

Who would have ever thought that my husband and brother would become such good friends? Chris had visited my brother several times on his trips to California and later bought a Bronco from him. They have a certain kinship with their love for their classic Ford Broncos and, of course, they lived happily ever after.

The wedding is over now, and I had accomplished something I never thought I would. A funny story I have to share about our honeymoon: as I said before, we did not have much money between the two of us, so we did what we could. We would go to the casinos with our nickel rolls, sit and drink for free, find the cheapest buffets to eat at, and even attend a time-share pitch for the free meal and gifts. It was time for Chris to leave, and he had to turn in our rental car. Well, we were out of money by this time, so I told him to say he was heading to Iraq for the conflict going on there. That was enough, they compted him for the car and all was good.

We were given a cashier's check as a gift from Chris's family, and it was time to cash it for some more spending cash. This was going to be difficult for us. There was nowhere to cash it. We were given the name and place of a guy who would do it for us. We took the address and our $100 check and headed out. Things were starting to get a little scary. We were now in a very sketchy alley way and there were only a set of metal stairs leading to the second floor. We ventured up and sitting in a dark office behind a large desk was a man who looked like a mafia boss. What were we in for here? He kindly cashed our check, took a small fee and sent us on our way. Still, we get a good laugh out of this story.

I am now 26. I was married, but the predictions I had made early on for myself, would they come true? Would I live to see forty? Now that I'm married, would we ever have children? So many questions. I always tried to live in the present, but these questions had always plagued me. Would I ever meet the right man? I did just that! There were so many unknowns in my life.

Chapter 6: The Challenges After Marriage

Chris was now back from Okinawa, and we were off to our first duty station together. It was a whole new world for me! Jacksonville, North Carolina. I had never moved out of my parents' house. This was all new for me. I purchased our furniture and all our household goods after I returned from Reno. My parents bought us a washer and dryer set and gave us some of my old bedroom furniture. They even gave us their old dining room table and chairs. We rented a cute little two-bedroom duplex, and I set it up so nicely.

We had several visitors. Chris's family and mine. Chris met another one of my sisters while we lived there. Shortly after moving to NC, Chris received orders to deploy to the Mediterranean for 6 months. What was I going to do? I've never had to manage everything on my own. I never lived alone either. I learned quickly, though. There were times when money was so short, I bounced checks, yes, one time to the Girl Scouts for cookies. I wasn't spending a lot of money, but we had different spending habits, and I was unaware of his spending out at sea. He was also going into different countries' ports. I made it work, though. I was okay with being alone. I also became the money handler for us. I had my own little system, paying the rent and bills on time and handling the financial woes that would arise. I was able to put money aside for future vacations. I became very good at handling what money we did have.

Upon Chris's return, we finally started a life as a married couple. We would go and play pool often because it was something we could afford. I had learned to use woodworking tools with my father, so we decided to make our own living room furniture. It was all in a southwestern pattern to go with all the quilts and wall hangings I had made while Chris was in Okinawa. The furniture wasn't the best. The entertainment center was even a little lopsided, but we were proud of it. We spent a lot of quality time together on those projects.

The first four years of our marriage went well. A few hypoglycemia incidents and a few hospitalizations because of DKA. The first one was a peptic ulcer after I returned from our elopement. Another one from a kidney infection. Happiness was all I felt at this time. I had someone with me going through these episodes with, and they didn't scare him away.

We were now on our second move and new duty station. We got orders back to Virginia Beach. The first year back in Virginia was an easy one. We had moved into a nice 2-story townhouse that was close to Chris's work. Very convenient. I decorated this home so nicely. Interior design was my hobby. If I were going to move every three years with my military guy, I would have many homes to decorate.

It was our second year in that townhouse, and somehow, I fractured my big toe on my right foot. This probably happened while going up and down the staircase, like with my left foot years prior. I wasn't sure how I broke it. Chris got me to an Orthopedic Surgeon who specializes in diabetic foot care. My toe was now swollen three times its normal size and in horrible pain. Surgery was next for me; my toe got pinned and later cast. After a few weeks, during my recovery, I noticed some more than the usual pain. The next day, my toe had blown up and looked very infected. Again, three times its normal size. We returned to the surgeon, and I got the news that I had developed a bone infection called osteomyelitis. This was caused by the pin placed in the toe. The surgeon sent me to an infectious disease doctor who put me on a six-week IV antibiotic cycle. This was extremely scary for me. It brought back one of the things I was told during those first lessons about my disease. Is this going to lead to an amputation? Things like that are always on my mind with diabetes.

My toe healed nicely. It was almost six weeks after my antibiotic cycle had finished when I started feeling ill. My foot swelled up and looked horrible. I developed several open areas on the bottom of that foot. This was still the right foot. We returned to my Orthopedic Surgeon, and he informed me that the foot had several broken bones and would need to be reconstructed. So, I agreed to have another surgery. My diabetes was not under control at this time. With diabetes, any type of infection can throw the sugars into an upward pattern. I was taking so much insulin, trying to get my sugars back into control. This was without any success. Surgery was scheduled again. This time for an entire foot reconstruction. Would I survive this? Could I survive this?

First on my surgery agenda was the reconstruction of my right foot. Then the surgeons took out my left hip bone and took out half of my foot, the infected part. They replaced the missing part of the foot with the hip bone. They did this with several screws and pins. I had to have my Achilles tendon shortened next. My right lower leg and foot were so scarred up. Stitches and staples are everywhere. I also had stitches in my left hip. It was not a pretty sight. I felt ugly. Chris helped me through all this and never made me feel undesirable. I had scars on top of the other scars. My right leg was now slightly shorter than my left leg, and I could no longer move my toes or my ankle. I was a mess after this. I had so much support from the people in my life that I was getting along pretty well. What's next? Would I heal from this?

While I was healing from the foot surgery, my eyes started giving me some scary issues. I started getting treatment for Diabetic Retinopathy. The condition that causes blindness in diabetics. My treatments included thousands of laser shots in both eyes. Some of the laser shots hit the part of my eyes that helped with night vision. Just one more diabetic complication I would now have to deal with. My body was fighting me. I was no longer in control. This brought it all back to me. Those early lessons I was being taught about my disease. Who would have ever guessed I would be faced with so many complications of this horrific disease? Not me.

Now I have one leg shorter than the other, and I can no longer see at night. It seemed to have become a never-ending battle for me. This disease is a beast! Not only was my physical being affected, but it was also taking a psychological toll on me.

As my recovery progressed, I started to get that familiar sensation. My foot swelled up again, and spots had opened on the bottom of my foot. These openings were called diabetic ulcers, and my foot hurt beyond belief. Back to the surgeon, we headed. My body had rejected the hardware for a second time. I had developed another osteomyelitis. This time, to have all the hardware removed and another round, six weeks of IV antibiotics. My foot was now deformed. It didn't even look human. I was missing several bones and several surgical scars from the many stitches I received. I developed an awful limp. Oh yeah, I was also losing my eyesight at the same time this was all going on. I was done with this, but I had to continue my journey because I had a husband, and he was on this journey with me. Plus, I wasn't ready to give up. I've never been that person. I was now 29 years old. I had been married for some time now. There was something missing in my life. I continued to run my home daycare, but I started to desire something else. A child of our own. I wanted to be a mother!

Chapter 7: My Dream Realized

Those last two years were tough on me. I buckled up and moved on yet again. New orders with the military came in for Chris. We packed our household goods again and headed back to North Carolina. We were now in a healthy financial position to buy our first home. We found the nicest tiny single-family home with three bedrooms and two bathrooms in a nice area of Jacksonville. The purchase was made. We were now homeowners. I felt like an adult. Just one more part of my life I had never imagined would happen.

Shortly after we moved down to Jacksonville, North Carolina, I was approved to be placed on an insulin pump. I was so excited! This was something I had heard about, and it would replace all the shots I was taking. I took at least 10 shots a day. The constant need for insulin shots was an all-day, everyday endeavor for me. I was tired and felt I was tied to the house. After being placed on an insulin pump, I was able to keep my blood sugar in reasonable control. Being tighter control also helped with my healing. I had finally recovered from my foot ordeal, and my eyes were improving. I still couldn't see well enough at night to drive, though. This was a significant loss for me. That insulin pump gave me a lot of hope for how my life was going to be from now on.

Our lives were moving along smoothly. No new struggles to face for a while. Some news was given to me at a routine doctor's appointment. I was pregnant. This couldn't be. The doctors, right away, said that this could eventually kill me. It would destroy my kidneys, and I should consider ending the pregnancy. I wasn't very far along yet. Together, we all agreed to do what needed to be done. My kidneys were already showing signs of damage. This whole scenario reminded me of a movie I had seen before called "Steel Magnolias." I remembered what eventually happened to the main character. Was this the story of my life?

After the loss of the child, the one we made together, I had a one-track mind. I really wanted a child of our own. It took several months to get over this loss, but I was determined. I was going to make this challenge into another triumph.

I put all my heart, soul, and time into the adoption process. I had to find a reputable Adoption Agency first. I found a Christian one located in Atlanta, Georgia. After speaking with the agency supervisor, I was hooked. I read all the available references. Okay, the agency was decided upon, and I jumped right into the next steps. First, and foremost, I needed a medical clearance from my endocrinologist. No problem. He was just pleased that I was doing this through adoption and not naturally. We needed to head to the local police station and get our driving records and our security clearances. No problem with that. We were both law-abiding citizens and good drivers. Next, we got our financial records and credit scores. No problem. Because of all my tight bookkeeping, we were in a good financial state. Time for us to fill out the application and inform the agency on what sex, race, and age of the child we were interested in adding to our family. I told our agent that we only wanted a newborn. We were asked if we wanted to do an open or closed adoption. I said closed. The next question came from me. I asked, "What type of child becomes available the quickest?" I was told that bi-racial boys were our quickest route. I replied, "Then that's what we want."

My next steps were to prepare our Life Book and prepare a letter to the birth mother. I made a beautiful book for her. I filled it with photos of all our family members. We both had a lot of those photos to add. There were several photos of Chris and me together, including our wedding photo. The book was filled with fun photos. I used stickers to add to the aesthetics. I added photos of our house and vehicle. It was put together with such care. A real show-getter.

It had been coming up on a year since everything in the adoption process was completed and sent off to the agency. Several copies of our life book and letters to the birth mothers, and now the waiting game had begun. One month later, I got that call. The best call I have ever received! I was told that we were chosen by a couple who loved the life book I had put together, and they were having their child in one week. The big question: "Do you want this child?" I said, "Yes, of course."

My excitement was unbelievable. I called Chris at work right away, and all I could get out was a tearful, "We were chosen"! He was clueless as to what I meant. After I explained it all to him, his excitement grew and he put in his leave papers and applied for the loan.

We had one week to prepare. I had already set the nursery up with the help of my mother. It was all primary colors and with a farm animal theme. My mother was very artsy. She made several farm animals in overalls. She made the curtains and a wall hanging. I bought several clothing items and was also gifted with several outfits, diapers, and formula, and of course, the car seat and stroller. We were ready.

I was in a state of elation, and when we got into my parents' car, it all became our reality. We were going to Georgia to get our son. He was going to be coming home with us. It took us all day to get to Georgia. We arrived in Savannah late in the evening. We stayed the night there with my best friend and her husband. I had chosen them to be our son's Godparents. They gladly accepted. We had a nice dinner and talked about all the things we were expecting to happen in his life. I did not sleep that night. The excitement was unreal!

Off we went to Conyers. The city the birth parents were from. Before we left for our drive, together we put the car seat, rear facing in the middle back seat. I was aware of how to do this because of my daycare days, and taking the babies, I watched with me everywhere. We arrived in Conyers, just outside of Atlanta, got our room, and got dressed up. Later that night, we met at The Outback restaurant, connected to the hotel we were staying at. Our adoption agent and the birth parents joined us. The birth was scheduled for the next morning. She would be having a C-section. This was because of her medical condition. The dinner was extremely difficult for me. I had a problem with making eye contact with her. I even talked through our agent, instead of asking her questions straight out. My heart sank at the end of our dinner. The last question the birthmother asked was, "What if I change my mind"! All I wanted at that point was a drink. I asked Chris to order me one at the bar. Could I handle her changing her mind at the last minute? Please don't let that be our reality. Another sleepless night.

Morning could not have gotten there sooner. We got up, dressed, brushed our teeth, and went off to the hospital. The birth had already taken place, so we headed straight to her hospital room. It was a very awkward moment for us all. I couldn't wait to get out of there and go see our son. We had chosen the name Tyler David. Chris picked the middle name, David, from the bible. Finally, that time had come, and we were brought to the nursery window. A nurse held up our son, Tyler David. He was the most beautiful baby I had ever seen. I couldn't wait to hold him now. We were then led to a nursery room to be with our amazing child. His birth weight was 6 pounds, 7 ounces. He was 21 inches long and had big brown eyes. He didn't have much hair, so we could only wonder what kind of hair he would eventually end up with. His color was a beautiful light tan. Similar to my coloring. We spent the entire day with him, not even taking a break to eat. I am now a mother! Chris is now a father! From a tragedy to a very big triumph. That wonderful day was May 21, 1998.

Tyler was released from the hospital the next day, and we did the handover from our agent in the Burger King parking lot. It made for a cute picture. Policy does not allow the handover to be done on hospital grounds. We were more than happy to go across the street to do this. We placed Tyler in his car seat. Thankfully, he was asleep for this. We drove back to Savannah with this little child in the car with us. I would not leave the back seat. He wasn't a fan of the car seat, but we learned pretty early on that he loved the swing we were given by my best friend. Sleeping was difficult for me. I just wanted to stare at him, especially when he was sleeping. Guess I had some first-time mother jitters as well. It was all worth it. I put my whole heart into this process, and I was so prepared for the gift of motherhood.

After several weeks, in a run-down extended stay motel, we were able to leave the state of Georgia and return to our home in Jacksonville, North Carolina. While in the motel, one day this little girl walked past our open window singing, "I love sex and candy." That song became Tyler's birth song. We laugh about that to this day. We were ready to leave. This could not have been the best time for us either. We had gone through all our finances, and it was time for Chris to return to the base. We did make one stop on our way out. That was to introduce Tyler to my best friend and her husband, his chosen Godparents. They were so happy for us.

Now three things have happened in my life that I never could have imagined. I was in a great marriage, I was finally able to control my diabetes, and I had become a mother. I had learned to build strength within myself. I was not going to let whatever was in store for me hold me down. I could survive anything thrown my way. I had thus far, and I would have much more in store for me. With everything going right in my life, I was concentrating on my physical wellness. My diabetes was well controlled, and I was doing great. Was there still more in store for me? I could never have imagined what would be next. Would I be able to survive anything else?

Chapter 8: The Biggest Challenge Yet

Motherhood was everything I had dreamed it to be. My marriage was on good grounds. My health was in very good shape. I had gotten used to having a deformed foot and walking with a bad limp. The funny thing was that Tyler started walking and mimicked my limp. We looked cute walking next to one another. I was killing it and feeling great while I was doing it!

Our three years in Jacksonville were up, and it was time to have our household goods packed and take on a new set of orders. That rinse and repeat cycle. This time, we were heading to Dallas, Texas, for Chris to do recruiting duty. We decided to drive cross-country for this move. We had two vehicles at this time: Chris's Bronco and my Corolla. We packed the Corolla with what we needed to live with for a few months, food, and our essential paperwork. The Corolla was attached to the Bronco and off we went. This trip was a very difficult one for us. The Bronco was lifted high off the ground, and I had to get in and out of the truck on my own. Sometimes Tyler is in my arms.

It was day two of our trip, and first, the bronco was not running well. We pulled into an auto shop and got the part needed for the truck. Chris fixed the problem, and we were off again. Day three, I started having incidents of high blood sugar, and I noticed my foot was hurting. This was my right foot again. My foot started swelling up, and my blood sugar was getting higher. I couldn't control it. I started getting very nauseous. I knew what this meant. I was going into diabetic ketoacidosis, my foot was broken, and I was developing an infection. I was done!

The trip had finally come to an end. We had planned to live with Chris's brother and his wife until we found a place of our own. I continued to get sicker and sicker. My foot exploded. Off we went to the hospital in this strange town. I was right. My foot was infected again. I thought I was over all these infections. I was brought into surgery. The doctor told me he did not know whether he could save my foot. All I could think of was what did this mean for Tyler? After the anesthesia wore off, the first thing I did was look down. Luckily, my foot was still there, but with another chunk of bone removed, leaving it even more deformed. There was also another bone infection that needed to be treated with IV antibiotics, and I was to be non-weight bearing on that foot. We were staying in a three-story house, with us on the second floor. I had to figure this out. Chris was at his new job, and I had a lot of appointments to get to. I drove with my left foot and was on crutches until I got a wheelchair. Tyler was two, and I had all these appointments. Thank God he was the most well-behaved child during this time. We made it work. Chris had to leave town for a week when I returned from the hospital, so I was pretty much on my own to figure this out. I had come up with some different maneuvers to get in and out of the car with Tyler. I had a one-track mind. I needed to find somewhere else to live.

It took six weeks for me to recover from this surgery. We found an apartment complex to move into in a nearby town. Thankfully, it was on the first floor. Everything was going better for me, and I was weight-bearing once again. I used the gym at our complex. Tyler and I also got a lot of use out of the pool. I would use the treadmill after Chris returned from work. Then, on the treadmill one day, that awful feeling returned to my foot, and it felt like the same symptoms. So, I go back to the doctor. I had developed another bone infection, only this time in a different area of the foot. I went back to surgery. No IV antibiotics this time, though, just oral ones. I had another piece of bone removed and was non-weight-bearing for another six weeks. Tyler and I continued our daily routines. I took him everywhere with me. He would ride on my lap in the wheelchair. I would have fun with him, so I was not thinking about the condition; I was focused on Tyler. I took him to play at the playground in our apartment complex. All this from my wheelchair. I was making it work.

I couldn't believe I had made it through this one. I was thinking I was finished, but no. This cycle continued happening. The broken bones and infections. Two more times for me. Finally, my doctor told me there was nothing else he could do for my foot. He told me it couldn't be up to him to decide this, but I needed an amputation. That had to be my decision. I asked him if he felt I would be strong enough to use a prosthetic leg. He said he felt good about it because I was young and had the right attitude. He also saw how I maneuvered with Tyler. I made that decision. Time to end this cycle and have my foot and lower leg amputated. I have now turned 36 years young.

The surgery date was scheduled, the hospital was booked, and I had informed all the family what I was about to have done. The surgery was scheduled for March 14, 2001.

I had my surgery as scheduled, and everything went as planned. The first thing I did after waking up was look down. It was hard to take in at first. The mood soon changed. Tyler had come to visit along with Chris. He was so happy to see me, then jumped right on top of me, nearly missing my leg. He brightened everything up for me. I love that boy. My mother arrived that night. Chris's father was also there before going back to Michigan. I was a little shy about allowing others to see me so soon after losing my leg.

I got up on crutches right away, on the first day. I was proud of myself; no time to wallow in what had become of my leg. When my mother came into the hospital to see me, I was going down the hall with the physical therapist. My mom said she was shocked, but saw me smiling, and she knew I would be alright. I was amazed at myself, so were my therapists. I told myself I had this. Just get me home so I can learn my new routine.

We had moved out of the apartment and into a house prior to my surgery, so getting around would be easier for me. My sister and niece joined my mom and stayed for several weeks with me during my recovery. During this recovery time, Chris and I had our tenth wedding anniversary. We went to a Greek restaurant and to the movies. This was my first time out since my surgery, and

I was extremely uncomfortable being out. It had only been ten days since the surgery. Several days later, we all went into downtown Dallas and ate at a very crowded restaurant. To get through the crowded tables with the giant white cast, all the attention was on me. My anxiety was horrific. I just wanted to crawl into a hole and hide. The humor took me a while, but it eventually returned. It took two months until my leg would fully heal, and I would receive my first prosthetic leg.

During my healing time, and before getting my leg, I had become my old self. I would take Tyler everywhere with me. We did the grocery shopping, and I would push the cart from my chair and use my left leg to move myself down the aisles. I would take Tyler up to the park daily. He would ride his bike there, and I would wheel in my chair, one leg and all. I would crawl all over the jungle gym with him, even push him on the swings. He would always be too tired to ride his bike back home, so I would hook it to the back of my chair and wheel home with him on my lap. We were quite a sight to see. Tyler was also attending all my doctor appointments, and he enjoyed our trips out. It had become the day for the staples to be removed from my incision site. Tyler was up on the examining table by my side, so interested in what was taking place. My doctor asked Tyler if he would like to help. This thrilled him, and he pulled out several of the staples. What an amazing experience for this young boy.

It was on one of our park trips, and another mother was watching me. She approached me and said she saw me with Tyler and asked me if I would be interested in watching her two kids part-time. I had mentioned to her earlier in our conversation that I had done home daycare for years. So, I took on watching her two children and sometimes a third. Tyler was happy to have other kids at the house to play with. I continued watching her kids until the end of the school year.

I now had my new leg and was getting along very well. I became extremely homesick. Chris was always busy with his job and taking trips. He was also working on his bachelor's degree. The company was what I truly needed. I told Chris I was going to take Tyler and go back to Virginia Beach for a few weeks. My best friend was also going to be in Virginia, and I was going to surprise her for her baby shower. I was back with my friend's group and my parents. I was so proud of myself. I had just gotten a new prosthetic, and I traveled from Dallas with a two-year-old all on my own. This was another triumph for me.

Next on my agenda was to get Tyler enrolled in preschool. I found a great school very near our house. He needed to be around other kids full-time. I was killing this mother role with one real leg and one false leg. What are we in store for next?

Chapter 9: Defying The Odds

2001 was a very eventful year. My amputation, Tyler turned three and started Preschool, and the biggest event of that year was the attack on America. There were several planes hijacked and used as missiles to bomb the Twin Towers in New York City. One plane was used to bomb The Pentagon, and the last plane crashed in a field in the state of Pennsylvania. The USA was now at war. Chris was continually working on getting his bachelor's degree. We were still living in Texas, and I was getting used to having my new prosthetic leg. My new leg was starting to feel more like my real leg. Any slight touch would give me the sensation of an actual touch to real skin. It felt like my toes were being squashed together when I had a sock and a shoe on the prosthetic. I was very happy with getting a fake skin cover on this leg. It not only looked real, but it also made me psychologically feel it was real and natural. There were also the pains and pangs that go along with this leg. The nerve damage was intense. I deal with what's called phantom pain. At times, it was as intense as the newly amputated leg.

Dealing with the shame and not liking what I saw when I looked down at my half leg took me a while to get past. I did not like taking my prosthetic off. I even slept with it on at first. The grief I was feeling for Chris as well, and how he was feeling about having a wife with only one leg was overwhelming for me. He would tell me that it didn't matter to him, but I had a hard time accepting that. I felt all my medical issues, and the scope of what had become of my health, made me a big burden for him, and now the loss of my right leg. Tyler also dealt with some remarks from other kids at the park. They would point and call my leg a robot leg. I would tell him that these kids think it's cool and they wish their moms had a robot leg. These feelings started to take over my every thought, but I knew I had to move on and remember my biggest purpose. That purpose was to be the best mother I could be for Tyler and to continue being a good wife who would always step up and do my part.

It was now 2002, and it was March. I suggested to Chris that we spend a family day at Dave & Busters. The day was going great! We were having so much fun doing our family day, and Tyler was winning all the games. We had a wonderful lunch when we first arrived there. I had taken my insulin coverage, via my insulin pump, and my carbohydrate count. I have become extremely proficient with this whole process. We were there for over four hours playing all the games. Tyler was getting tired. Chris also had plans to go to the library with his brother that night to do some schoolwork. It was bittersweet, but this day had to end.

We returned home and went inside. Tyler and I were resting in the lounge chair in our living room. Tyler fell asleep immediately. Chris left the house to go pick his brother up, and shortly after he left, my blood sugar began to drop. I don't remember anything after that.

Chris returned several hours later that night. He noticed that things were a little off. He noticed the garage door was open, and one of our dining chairs was under the garage door opener on the inside of the inner garage wall. When he came into the house, he saw Tyler on the floor next to me playing with his Power Ranger toys. He noticed I was foaming at the mouth, in the posturing position. He called the paramedics but also tried to raise my blood sugar. Some other things he noticed were that Tyler had tried giving me juice. The juice was all down the front of my blouse. He saw a rock and a butter knife on the floor. The juice bottle was new, and he told Chris he got these items to open the bottle of juice. The rock was to sharpen the knife. Tyler and I used to sharpen sticks with rocks in our backyard all the time. He had also tried to call 911, and his message was recorded but not sent. He calmly said, "I need help. My mommy is sick." It killed me to hear the stories of that day. My poor son was alone with me as I was dying. This event will surely make a big difference in his later life.

The paramedics could not get my blood sugars up. I had been given D50, glucose via IV, with no results. I was loaded into the ambulance and transported to the nearest hospital. I was in a deep diabetic coma. All this was going on, and I was totally unaware of it.

There were several doctors brought in to be on my case. They tried to find a reason for what was going on. With all the glucose I had been given by the paramedics, Tyler, and Chris, that day, my levels should have risen. They did not rise up in the slightest. The Endocrinologist had no explanation for why this had happened. The neurologist did all sorts of tests on my brain and declared me to be brain-dead. I had been in this state for three days with no changes to my condition. Chris contacted my family. Together, they all decided to shut off the life support and stop the medications I was getting. My two younger sisters had flown in from Arizona, and while all life support was being shut off, my sister, the funny one, leaned down in my ear and told me to, "wake the FUCK up!" I tried to slap her face. My younger sister had seen me twitch, and I squeezed her hand. I did this apparently because of a joke she tried to make.

By some miracle, I started to breathe on my own. My eyes opened. I started asking for my baby boy. I was having a strange vision of an older couple walking away with him, and he was screaming. Tyler wasn't even at the hospital at this time. The doctors were called in, and they could not believe what they were seeing. There was no explanation for what I had just done. Chris called my family and gave them the unbelievable news of this miracle. My family all came to the consensus that I had nine lives. It's now a running joke amongst all of them. My endocrinologist mentioned that it may have been what is called an Addison Crisis. I had never been diagnosed with this autoimmune disorder but had been told that some type 1 diabetics contract other autoimmune disorders during their lives. That could be the answer to all my random low blood sugars that I experience.

I was released from the hospital the very next day. Good luck to you from the doctors and the staff. I experienced some short-term memory issues and could not keep my train of thought on track. There were issues with finding simple words. My mother, sister, and her daughter came and stayed with me during this time. I had several episodes of losing it altogether because I just couldn't remember what I was doing at certain times. The three of them were stepping in and helping with Tyler's care. They took him to his preschool and took care of him after school. I appreciated all they did during those times. I was in a desperate frame of mind. I had people who needed me just as much as I needed them.

I got back on track after a few months and returned to my old self. Doing all my wife and mother duties. What was in store for me now? I almost didn't make it to that forty-year mark. I was getting closer to it. There was so much more I wanted out of my life, and for Tyler's life.

I have not finished! I survived another near-death episode! The best way to do this was to take a trip to Hawaii with my family. Tyler would be there with several of his cousins, who were a month older than he was. Tyler is three now. This was an amazing trip for all of us.

Chapter 10: The New Addition

I survived another move and all the struggles that came with it. The lost items from our shipment of household goods, and some damaged items. These three-year tours were coming and going at what seemed like a very quick pace. We had now been married for eleven years and had weathered six moves. Tyler was four years old, and he was experiencing his second move. Moving time again. I was really going to miss our sweet little home. It was time for us to pack up our household goods again and move to a new duty station. Chris got orders back to Virginia Beach. I was so happy for us. We were near my parents again, and Tyler was going to have his grandparents as regulars in his life now. Being in a military family does take you away from family. I knew this all too well, both as a child and now as an adult.

Tyler and I traveled to Virginia Beach on our own prior to when Chris did his check-out with his job in Dallas. We found a cute three-bedroom rental home that was within walking distance of the elementary school Tyler would be attending. Tyler finished pre-school in the first year and started elementary school. Kindergarten here he comes!

A couple of years had passed, and he was now a six-years old and in the first grade. My home daycare was up and running, and I was again watching other people's children. This just lit that desire inside me. I was ready to add to our beautiful family with another child. I ran this idea past Chris, and he was happy that I was finding purpose again. I had a new forty-year goal. This time it was to adopt our second child. Forget just living to be forty. I knew what I wanted, and I went full force to accomplish this goal.

The adoption process had started again for me and Chris. This time, Tyler will take part in it as well. He was excited to be a help. This also gave him an insight into how adoption worked. I contacted the same agency in Georgia. I filled out the application, stating that we desired another bi-racial newborn boy. This worked so wonderfully for us the first time, why try fixing what ain't broke? The same next steps in the process were completed, and our package was sent off to the agency. The life book had to be updated, though. Pictures of Tyler were added, and some new pictures of our additional family members. After I completed the life book, the wait began. Just waiting for that wonderful call to let us know we had been chosen. I was so ready for this. It brought me such joy, and I felt my purpose had returned even more than before. We would be adding another child to our family and raising this child as he deserved.

We had been notified right away, but the birthmother's family decided they would raise this child. This had happened early in our adoption process, so it hadn't quite sunk in yet that this could be our next child. It must have been right when the agency received our package. We were now entering our seventh month in the waiting, and the call came. There is a birthmother expecting a mixed boy, and she is due in two months. "Are you interested in this child?" I let them know that

YES, we were and looked forward to working with this birthmother. Several calls between us were being made, and she was informing us about all that was going on with her and the baby. We were told everything from the due date to the expected weight and, of course, the sex of the child. The excitement we felt was unbelievable. The fact that she was taking care of herself and this child gave us such hope.

We were at the nine-month mark now, and we were called by our agent to say that the baby would be arriving any day. This excitement was unreal. Tyler was so thrilled to be getting a full-time baby added to our family. He was always thrilled when the babies were at the house that I cared for. Chris went to work the next day and submitted his leave papers. I had been setting up the nursery in the rental home we were living in at this time. Planes, trains, and automobiles were the themes. The perfect boy décor. There were a few baby furniture pieces leftover from Tyler, so those were used, and I purchased some adorable boy clothes. We, again, were given some baby items from family and friends. Our church put on a baby shower for us as well. We were prepared for our little baby boy to come and become a member of our beautiful family.

Time to get our second child. Our vehicle was packed, and we were off to Savannah to stay with my best friend until the birth of our second son. Such is the feeling of deja vu. Making that drive to stay with the same friends in Savannah and waiting for the call. On the drive, we reached South of the Border, North Carolina, and into South Carolina. I received a call from our agent. Was I ready for this call? We were informed that our birth mother had been falsifying all the information and had received no prenatal care. I questioned if she was even pregnant. The next news we received was even more shocking. She was expecting a girl. The baby was not showing any signs of medical issues, so the ultrasound looked healthy. They could not tell us the expected due date, though. Again, the question came, "Did we want this child?" I looked over at Chris, his mouth and eyes dropped. He looked like he was going to be sick. I said, "Of course, we do." Tyler had heard all that was going on and said from the back seat, "I always wanted a sister." That solidified it for us, and all was going to be fine. It was meant to be by the grace of God.

The next call I made was to my parents about bringing our daughter home. My father said, "He always saw me as a girl mom." My mother told me she would run out and get some girl décor for me to redo the room. I was very appreciative of them. I was even more appreciative of this little baby girl we would make our daughter.

We arrived at my best friend's house in Savannah. The first thing I asked her was to take me shopping. We went to a Carter's outlet store and got all I would need for our baby girl. My friends have two daughters, and most generously, let me go through the clothes boxes they had saved from their baby days.

I had chosen the name Cory Michael for our new son. Thank God I had already chosen a girl's name years prior. I always used to say if I ever had a girl, this would be her name, Kari Marie. A beautiful name for what our beautiful daughter will be.

It was our third night in Savannah when, at 3:00 AM, a call came in that the birth mother's water had broken, and we needed to get to a small town called Douglas, still in Georgia, as soon as possible. We loaded up our car and got Tyler up. We would have about a four-hour drive. Tyler was not his usual happy self. He was acting a little strange and came off frightened. When I asked him what was wrong, he said he didn't want us to give him back. It was hard to hear him feel that way, but I jumped into the reassuring mother and knew exactly what to say to him. I told him we would never do that, and we were just going to get him his little sister. I told him he was always my baby boy, and nothing would ever change that. He looked relieved to hear those words and fell right back to sleep.

The day was July 19, 2004. It was around 8:00 AM when we arrived in Douglas and immediately went to the birthing part of the hospital. This was the first time I had seen her birthmother. She matched the description I was given in every way. The doctor was in the room as well, looking a little frustrated. He was trying to get information on the mother's prenatal doctor. Our agent finally informed the doctor about the lack of prenatal care, but informed him she had gotten an ultrasound earlier and all was good with the baby. Looking very upset at this point, the next question asked was directed at me. "Who are you?" I told him I was the adoptive mother, and my husband was in the hallway with our son. His following statement was that the wait would not be long, and he'd be inducing her and getting us our baby ASAP. I appreciated him.

Chris and Tyler came into the room to meet our birthmother. They decided to go grab a few things at a convenience store, while I stayed with her in the birthing suite. It was going on three hours since the induction and we were all getting antsy. I did one final walk around the halls with her, then it became that time. She was dilated enough to give her an epidural and start the birthing process.

The doctor came back in to check her. He stated that he was going to break her water and deliver our baby. I was a little confused because she had said her water had already broken. I got the feeling our doctor was done working with her and wanted to be done with this birth. It was hard to hear all the falsehoods we were being told during our time working with her and with our agent. There was no taking her to appointments or looking at her records. Not even getting the OBGYN she was supposedly working with. This was all water under the bridge at this point. The doctor, so kindly, asked me if I wanted to be there for the delivery. I was so excited and started crying as I said yes. I couldn't believe this. I was going to witness Kari being brought into this world.

Chris and Tyler were back, and I told them it was time, and I was going to stay in the room and be present for Kari's birth. This was all new for me, but I was more than excited to be there to witness my daughter's birth. They were excited for me. Tyler asked if he could stay, too.

It was that time now. I instructed her to breathe, to push, and I held her hand through the birth. The doctor lifted Kari up for me to see, and she was brought to the nurses to clear her lungs. She weighed 7 lbs. 14 ounces and was 20 inches long. Her skin was an exquisite brown, and her hair was black, but not much of it. One of the nurses went out of the room and had Tyler push the lullaby button to announce a new birth. He will remember that forever. When I came out of the room, I saw Chris and Tyler and could only say, through all my tears, "She's beautiful."

And that she was!

Having Kari in the family was so much fun. Tyler loved his little sister so much. I would go into her room to get her out of the crib on many occasions, and Tyler would be lying in the crib with her. They took their evening baths together, and Tyler even wanted to change her diaper. He changed her first diaper in the hospital after her birth. He was an amazing brother. We were all thrilled for Kari's first Christmas. She was now five months old, and my niece was getting married in Marco Island, Florida. She wanted to include all her cousins in the ceremony, including Kari. This was going to be our introduction of our beautiful daughter to my family. We always had such fun with my family, and it was great for all the little cousins to spend Christmas together. Several of the cousins were about the same age as Tyler. I liked to show Kari off. Every Friday, I would grab some Wendy's, go to Tyler's school with Kari, and have lunch with him and his class. This made him feel special because it was every Friday, rain or shine. I remember when we were still in Savannah, and this was with both Tyler and Kari's adoptions; they were only days old, and people would ask how old they were. We would say two or three days old. The looks we received were hilarious.

I would get the "Wow, you look amazing." I would just say Thank You. We always got a great laugh out of it.

This beautiful addition to the family happened prior to that infamous age of forty, and I had even more to live for now. I am starting to see the patterns in my life. All these challenges I faced after my diagnosis became my even bigger triumphs.

I had a beautiful family of my own. Even though we weren't the perfect family in any way, I've never seen us in any other way; I couldn't imagine it any other way. I was happy! My family was happy!

Chapter 11: Doing It All on My Own

Chris's tour in Virginia Beach has come to an end. We were off again. Packing the household goods, but this time, there was a vacation planned before we moved back down to the house in Jacksonville. We would be going back to a familiar place. These two places seemed to be our three-year routine. Virginia Beach, Jacksonville, Virginia Beach, back to Jacksonville. We were looking forward to visiting with family in Hawaii. Before our vacation and the traveling day, my parents put us up at their house after our household had been packed up. Kari was now ten-months and Tyler was six. We were going back to Hawaii again with both kids this time. It was going to be an introduction of Kari to some of my family members. We loved Hawaii and were very excited to get the chance to go there again.

The night before we left for the airport was a scary night for us. Chris had gone down to our house in Jacksonville to finish putting in the hardwood floors. My parents had left earlier for their flight, and we were flying out the next morning. I experienced one of my random low blood sugars. Tyler was becoming a pro at taking care of these incidents. It was just me and the two kids that night. When I was brought back and my blood sugar returned to normal, I realized there were several police and paramedics in the bedroom. I could hear Kari crying downstairs. Turns out, Tyler called 911 and saved the day. He's my little hero! The officers were so sweet to the kids. They gave Tyler a "Life Saving Award" for his heroics and gave Kari a little stuffed puppy. Tyler's award was presented to him at the police station in a nice ceremony. My parents were present for this award ceremony, and pride was beaming from us all.

These episodes are hard for me to get past. I have a hard time knowing I must rely so heavily on my young son to save me. I have become fearful of being left alone with them. No young child should be responsible for their parents. He has seen so much with his mother, and I hope he will remember the bad and replace it with the good in every situation. That is my goal with my kids.

Hawaii was another unforgettable vacation for us, and now that the vacation was over, we are off to our house in Jacksonville, time to start over again. Thank God we didn't have to find another home to rent. This is our own house. Just that alone was a heavy weight we didn't need to place on our backs with another move.

The house had been rented to several families before we returned to it. There was so much work that needed to be done. Together, we did a complete overhaul. I did the designing, and together we did the work. I had to give Chris the credit for doing all the painting. He did most of the construction work. I had to keep the kids entertained during those days. My design plan was spectacular. I redesigned our fireplace and had Chris tile the entire wall behind it. It was a one-of-a-kind fireplace. I chose the color schemes for every room. We finished the house, and it was amazing. Both kids had their own rooms. They had beautifully colored walls with themes. Tyler's was Tommy Hilfiger, and Kari's was a Hawaiian theme. They loved their new rooms. We were very proud of our accomplishments and making that home our home.

I got Tyler enrolled in school. It didn't take long before he made a bunch of new friends. Most of the kids lived in our neighborhood. Kari was not quite two years old yet, so she really didn't need friends. I continued our Friday lunches with Tyler. We had lived there before, so I knew some of the ladies in the neighborhood. It didn't take long before I met some other ladies. The neighborhood was full of good people.

A year had passed, and the war in Iraq was going strong. Chris was eager to be part of it there. We were not! Chris's orders were given to him, and he was heading to Fallujah, where he would be going as the General's Navy liaison. This overseas tour was scheduled to last 7 long months, his longest deployment yet. He was off again, only this time it was with the kids being at home alone with me. This one was going to be difficult. Would it all go well? Would he come back? Would my health hold up? Chris's departure deeply saddened the kids and me. It was now departure day, and we drove him onto the base. We said our tearful goodbyes, and he loaded the bus to take him to catch his flight. With the down feeling all around us, I decided I was going to treat the kids. We took a ride to the mall right after Chris drove off on the bus. It was up to them to get something they desperately wanted. Tyler wanted a gaming system, and Kari wanted her ears pierced. This little gesture brightened their spirits.

This wasn't his only deployment during our marriage. Chris was gone a lot. I survived two deployments, so one could say I was used to it. No, I wasn't. One of these deployments was on my own, and the other when Tyler was only six months old. The first deployment was six months long, and it was shortly after we first got married. These times were before cell phones, and regular phone calls were no such thing. I only talked with him twice, and both calls were only five minutes long. I was in the dark for much of that trip. Welcome to marriage with a military man. I guess I really didn't take notice of the time away with my father's military career. Maybe that's because I was just a child. Chris's second deployment was when Tyler was six months old. This was a three-month deployment, and it also fell during Tyler's first Christmas. I got used to these separations quickly. Did I really have a choice? I was hoping the kids would get used to his absence, too. But how can they? They were getting their first experience with an extended deployment, and it was in a war zone, so this was different from the short four-day weekend trips he had taken regularly throughout their childhood. There is no getting used to it.

Kari was three, and Tyler was nine, and we were in full deployment mode at home. We went on some fun adventures together. But there were always those feelings that something was missing. I tried to do something every weekend with the kids, sometimes even going on walks on base to explore. On several occasions, I drove back to Virginia Beach to visit with grandma and grandpa. Family members also came for visits. There were many school events going on at Tyler's elementary school, and I volunteered for many of these events. I got Kari enrolled in Preschool, and I would go to the gym on the days she had school. I never missed a field trip with either child. We had a great established routine. Christmas came and went. Birthdays and anniversaries as well. While Tyler was in school, Kari and I would have tea parties. She loved it when I made her my special quesadillas. I built plenty of toys for the kids. I did some major landscaping, even cutting back several trees. My biggest project was rehabbing the kitchen. I did the backsplash and put in new appliances. It turned out beautiful and matched the rest of the house. Our bedroom was next for me to conquer. The paint was redone, and I put up new molding. I loved using nail guns. If there were a festival in town or even near our town, I would load up the kids and let Tyler bring a friend, and off we would go. Never a dull moment for us. Thank God, my blood sugars stayed in control, and there were no 911 calls to be made. Kari had gotten a bad case of Croup that she just couldn't shake. She was sick for close to four weeks. Around this time, Tyler started to struggle with his schoolwork. I received several calls from his teacher. The school suggested that Tyler be evaluated for ADHD. The appointments were scheduled, and the testing was done. He scored high on the chart, but he was suffering from the attention deficit part of his diagnosis. The psychiatrist Tyler was working with tried medication. It worked for him at the time. We were getting through this and dealt with things as they came about. We were surviving and doing a great job at it! It's funny how life takes a turn, and you adjust to this new way of life. What would it be like with Chris home?

Upon Chris's return, the kids and I painted our front lawn with his welcome home greeting. We made signs and painted the van windows. Pizza and his favorite beer, Sam Adams, were waiting for him at home. Chris survived this deployment, and we survived his absence. We were all healthy. There were many things we had to catch up on. It was a relief to have him home and safe with us. A relief for all of us. However, there was a lot of getting used to having him there again. The kids would only come to me with any issue they were having; I was their go-to. If Chris told them to do something, they would come straight to me and ask if it was ok for them. The school wake-up routine was disturbed as well. It's the little things that were difficult to deal with, as any spouse or child experiences with the return from deployments. I became so independent with every little thing we did that Chris's way would take some getting used to again. We would do it, though. Having him home was much better than having him away.

Chapter 12: Here We Go Again

Another three years were up for us in Jacksonville. Rinse and repeat. Time to pack the household goods, find a new house, and get the kids enrolled in their appropriate schools. Chris's orders were just one hour outside of Jacksonville. Together, we made the decision to sell the Jacksonville house and move onto the Marine Base. We headed to Havelock, North Carolina. We sold our house to the first couple who toured it. It was an awesome house!

I was raised in base housing, and it was a wonderful part of my childhood. I was excited for the kids to experience this as well. The original house we were given was very old and in bad shape. Chris asked if I was ok with this house, and I said, "I'll make it work." Luckily, there were new houses being built, and we were first on the list to get one of them. The wait was well worth it. We spent the last two years of our three-year tour in this new, large house.

Chris had put on rank right before we left Jacksonville and was now the highest enlisted rank for the Navy. Again, he was the Navy liaison for a two-star Marine General. This job included constant trips, usually over the weekends, and more absences for the kids and me. I could sense the kids were over it. I knew I was.

The war was now in Afghanistan, and it was extremely volatile. The time came for Chris to accept orders to head into war again. The children were getting older. They understood the dangers of war now, and the children feared for their dad. We had experienced several service men and women losing their lives over there. Chris was on edge that night and wanted to get to the flight line right away. Tyler did not want him to leave again. Not one of us wanted that. Tyler was at that age when he needed a male around. He needed his dad. Tyler and Kari both had plenty of friends on base, and several were in the same situation they were. All these young men without having their fathers around. A lot of Mom's raising these young men. Every now and then we would see the black vehicle arrive at a home and shortly after the moving truck would be at that house. We all knew what that meant.

It was just the three of us doing the best we could. I was doing all the parenting duties, and we were surviving. This deployment was a year-long deployment. There would be an R&R two-week break at the six-month mark of this deployment. This meant more birthdays, anniversaries, and holidays without dad and husband at our side.

When Chris arrived in Afghanistan, he realized it was an ugly situation. He was losing sailors and Marines daily. That is a load for any hardcore military man or woman to handle. I could see him sinking with every Skype call. I wanted him out of there, and the kids just wanted Dad home.

The kids had a hard time speaking with Chris. Tyler never got the courage to speak with him. Repeatedly, Tyler would say that he didn't see Dad ever making it back home. I was starting to get that same feeling. Chris told me some pretty horrific stories about his experiences in this hellhole. Seeing and hearing about all the devastation was difficult to take. I always stayed positive in front of the kids, though. Again, I kept them occupied with their time. We always had new adventures to go on and places to go and check out. There was the usual base drama with some of the younger neighbors. Nothing too much for me, though. We made it work in our own way.

It was now the seventh month of Chris's deployment, and the month of our twentieth wedding anniversary. I placed my thoughts and fears aside and came up with a wonderful R&R trip for the whole family to enjoy. This will be the most memorable two weeks of our lives. Chris said he just wanted to be by the ocean. We just wanted him to come home. It didn't matter to us where we went, but this was going to be about Chris. I suggested we take a trip to Marco Island, Florida. In these plans, I wanted us to renew our wedding vows. I informed Chris of my plan, and he liked what I was laying down and I tried to get him involved with some of the planning as well. All of us were very excited about this trip.

My head started getting creative. Like with my adoption frame of mind. I was off and running. It was a great distraction from the war mess. I contacted the Chamber of Commerce in Marco. This was something they were excited to help me get accomplished for our family. They transferred me to one of their newspaper reporters, and a call was made to the reporter. I gave her a scenario of what I wanted to do for his visit. She liked what she heard and was willing to make it happen for us. A beach wedding. A lot of ideas were thrown my way.

This reporter wrote a very heartwarming story about everything from my health, our adopted children's story, all the missed anniversaries, birthdays, and Christmases, to the story of Chris's military career. This article was published when so many of the local businesses replied to the article and wanted to donate to us and our family. Restaurants, hotels, salons, photographers, bakers, and many more businesses donated. The beach wedding was a big surprise. The beach was decorated with a beautiful, flowered archway. There was a request for a song I would like to have sung. I chose "Marry Me" by Train. An acoustic guitar player would play and sing it for us.

A local fisher took Chris and Tyler on a fishing trip while Kari and I got our hair, nails, and toenails painted. They even arranged for us to have our makeup done. We looked so pretty! The Knights of Columbus were there, in full dress. Holding their swords in an arched walkway for us. It was paradise. It helped us all put Afghanistan behind us. My best friend and her family were our only guests. She has had a part in most of my major moments. I cherish her!

It all turned out to be wonderful for all of us. However, R&R was over, and it was time for Dad, Chris, to return to Afghanistan. This departure was harder than the first one. After he left, things started blowing up at home. Tyler developed an anger that was getting him in trouble at school. I got called in several times. He even got suspended from fighting. This was not his character at all. He was always a nice kid and helpful to everyone. He started to become confrontational, even with me. It was my job to calm him down, and I started having deep conversations with him. We always had an open relationship, and he was always able to tell me anything and everything going on in his life. He needed some deep counseling for the trauma he had gone through with both of his parents.

Tyler was now getting into some serious counseling. Regular counseling sessions were a weekly endeavor for us. That helped him with what he was going through with dad's absence and dealing with the what-ifs of Mom. This was also the age when a boy needs a male influence. He was getting interested in girls, and I took on the role of taking him to meet up with them. I would drop him off at parks and the movie theater on weekends. This helped some. I lived in a constant state of, What's next for us? Who would have guessed what was coming?

Hurricane Ophelia was heading straight for our town and the base. There were tornadoes, which were a big possibility for us as well. I prepared the best I could. I got gas in the car and made sure there was food in the house. Tyler and Kari went through that supply prior to the storm even hitting. The storm made a mess of the base. There were several tornadoes that came down, destroying a nearby subdivision. The electricity was out for almost four days. Several trees had come down across the power lines and our next-door neighbor's fence. A streetlight got taken out. Our neighborhood was cut off from the rest of the base, and we were stuck. On the second day, the lines and streets were cleared. Luckily, the power was restored at the front of the base. That meant so did McDonald's. Never ate so much McDonald's in my life. The kids were happy with that course of events. This was another event handled, and we came out of it fine. I was getting pretty used to this way of life, bringing a mess my way, and I always found a way to get through it. Of course, I had the help of the kids.

One day, I returned from doing a little shopping. Standing at our front door were two of Chris's fellow Master Chiefs. It was a Friday, so they were in their dress uniforms. My heart sank! I drove up into my neighbor's driveway and just sat there in the van. I was petrified! I couldn't move. They proceeded to walk up to the van. I rolled the window down, and they smiled and asked me how I was doing, and I chewed them out because I was terrified of what they might tell me. That still affects me to this day. I was sure we had lost Chris. Thank God that wasn't the situation. I told Chris about this, and he contacted them and told them to never do that again. They felt horrible putting me through that. All's forgiven.

It was the little things that were really weighing us all down. This was a base-wide effect. Tyler, Kari, and their friends, at a very impressionable age, were living in constant fear of losing their fathers and mothers. Times when kids need their fathers and mothers around.

Several of the wives and husbands at home doing it all were at their wits' end. Confused, misbehaving kids, and that constant "what next" feeling. What will today be like for me? What activity can I do with the kids this weekend to keep them occupied and their minds off their parents in a war? Never seemed like there would be a break in sight.

It was that time of the night for our Skype call. This was a great call. Chris told me he had been chosen to take orders to Hawaii, and that those orders would get him out of Afghanistan right before Christmas. He asked me if I was alright with these orders. Of course I was! The kids would have Dad home again just before Christmas, and they would get the chance to live in Hawaii. Things were looking up. I couldn't wait for them to come in through the front door.

The kids were living their lives similar to mine. Kari was the same age as I was when I first moved to Hawaii as a child. So, here we go again. Household goods got packed, arrangements were made for the trip, and we were off again. This was a sweet trip for us. First-class all the way. We felt like royalty. Life was good!

Chapter 13: Paradise Lost

The family was whole again. We landed in paradise, and the excitement for all of us was overwhelming. We were exhausted and couldn't wait to get to the hotel and crash. I was excited because the hotel we were staying in was the last hotel my family stayed in years ago when I moved back to the mainland and I was twelve years old at that time.

The hotel room was way too small for the four of us and all the luggage we had traveled with. Chris's new job was a pretty prestigious one, so getting us into nicer quarters was no issue. The house we were to move into was still occupied, and it would be a few months before we could move in. This worked for me, though. I got the kids enrolled in their appropriate schools. Kari was now in second grade, and Tyler was entering eighth grade. Chris was already on his first trip with his new boss and team. I got hooked up with my new endocrinologist and my new prosthesis. Upon Chris's return, I got my new car, and I was free to explore. So much has changed since I was there as a child. Everything was starting to feel aligned in our lives.

All I wanted to do was explore and show my husband and kids all the places I had gone, the things I had done, and tell them the stories. So many stories. They had all been here before, but now they were living here, in Hawaii, paradise!

Our first couple of years were good. My plan for the holidays was to spend our Thanksgiving on the other islands. The first year, we adventured to Maui. I arranged a helicopter tour for us to take during our trip. That was amazing. Everyone was thrilled with it. The trip was a big hit! The next Thanksgiving was spent on Kauai. Beautiful! We stayed in a very luxurious hotel. We did a day excursion tubing in the mountains, and I suggested we do a zipline trip next. Chris, Kari, and I went on this day trip. What an amazing thing for us to experience.

The adventures and the exploring continued back on our island. Chris was traveling a lot for work. Both kids had made good friends. Tyler was really into skateboarding, and so were his friends. The kids were going to the beaches and bodyboarding, surfing, and snorkeling. In Hawaii, there are many places to go and enjoy hiking, and the family took advantage of that. Kari started gymnastics and tennis. I made good friends with some of the neighboring ladies. We would go to the gym on Tuesdays and Thursdays. Things were good! I was happy, and so was the rest of the family.

Many of our family members were coming for visits as well. This gave Chris's family the chance to leave Detroit and visit our beautiful island.

It was now year three on the island. Tyler was in high school, and Kari was moving along in Elementary school. Chris was hard at work in his new position. I was doing my wife, and motherly duties. Keeping things straight and cleaning up messes.

There hadn't been any health issues going on with my life for some time. So far, so good! Then Tyler started having trouble in school. He started dating a local girl and hung out at the skatepark every night with the wrong group of kids. The calls from the school were coming in regularly. He was becoming disruptive in class and disrespectful to his teachers. He was later caught with some marijuana in his backpack and got suspended from school for two weeks. I hired a neighbor's college-age son to help with some tutoring. This went smoothly with him being home, but upon his return to school, his behavior worsened. The troubles ensued at school and in our home.

This behavior continued. He wasn't getting anything out of school. This was a sad thing because he was highly intelligent. What was going on with my son? I spoke with the school, and together we came up with a plan to have him drop out of school in his junior year. He would wait two months, and he could then take the GED test. We did precisely that. I made the appointment for him to take all four tests on Saturday. He passed all four subjects with flying colors. On to whatever was next in store for us.

Chris was getting to the end of his three-year tour in Hawaii. We started discussing what would be next. I was ready for him to retire, but that's not what was in store for us. The kids had had enough of the military life as well.

My health has been pretty good for several years. I was not ready for what hit me next. Another trip for Chris, and I started having all sorts of stomach pain and cramping. The pain one day became unbearable, so off I went to the base clinic. X-rays were taken, and it looked like I had an intestinal blockage. The doctor who saw me that day was worried about the images, though. She gave me a call later that evening and demanded that I go to the Army hospital. This was impossible for me to maneuver. It was nighttime, and I couldn't leave the kids alone in the house. I didn't know how long I would be there if I did leave. I also do not have any night vision. I brought myself to the hospital the next morning after the kids were off to school. Across the mountains I drove not even thinking about what was going on inside me. I turned my camera on and filmed the beautiful drive through the mountains. The waterfalls were amazing that morning. There was a CT scan already ordered for me upon my arrival. I got wheeled back to one of the bays in the ER and got into the hospital gown. Next was the contrast dye I had to drink, and next was the scan to be run. There was a mass spotted on my left kidney. That was all I was told. A referral was placed with the Urology clinic at this hospital. That was that. I waited for the referral to go through to the appropriate Doctor, and appointments were made.

Going to appointments on my own was a regular thing for me. I had no idea what was in store for me at the referral appointment: "You have cancer." The Physician's Assistant gave me that news. It was about twenty minutes later when the Urologist came in, and he confirmed what the PA had said. He informed me it was Renal Cell Carcinoma, RCC. I was very matter-of-fact. I calmly asked, "What does this mean for me now?" He explained to me the type of cancer, its size, location, and the course of action to be taken. This was all so much for me to listen to. I made another appointment. This appointment, I would have Chris there with me, and we could make the decision together on a course of action. Kari attended this appointment as well. She had to be with her momma. Having her there with us made me a little stronger.

Kari was getting ready to turn ten at this time. The doctor told me that surgery would be all I needed, and during the surgery, they would look for any markers to see if the cancer had metastasized or if chemotherapy would be needed. I just wanted to make sure Kari had the ice-skating birthday party she wanted and was so excited about. Thinking about what was in store for me was far from my mind until later that night. I had a party to organize, so after my big cry and calls to my family, my train of thought jumped the track, and I went all in on Kari's party.

The party was a great day for my little girl. Now it is back to taking care of me and this cancer. My diabetes was in great control, and my kidneys were still functioning fine despite the cancer. Not bad for someone living with Type 1 Diabetes for over thirty-seven years.

Let's do this! Deep down, I truly was very scared of what I was now facing, but I never showed it, though. The day of the surgery. I got to the hospital bright and early, got brought back to the pre-op section, was given full body wipes, a gown, a hair cap, signed the consent, had the IV placed, and off I went. This surgery lasted about 5.5 hours. I was told that it went very well and there were no markers to be found. There was no spread of the cancer. There was an issue with my blood pressure dropping during the surgery, but the Anesthesiologists were able to keep it safe for me. The ICU was next for me. This was just to keep an extra eye on my BP and diabetes, and it was also the only available bed for me. My surgeon let me know that if everything went well that night, I would be heading home the next morning. The goodbyes were said. Chris headed home to the kids, and I fell back into that anesthesia sleep.

There was so much chaos going on around me. Bells, buzzers, and whistles. Nurses and the Doctor in the ICU were scrambling all about. I was so confused. Was this all for me? There were a lot of drugs being pushed into my IV and a lot of medical terminology being thrown out there. I was still under anesthesia, so I was completely confused as to what was going on. Still not sure if it was because of me or another patient. Consciousness came and went with me during this time, so I was only getting bits and pieces as to what happened. My BP got dangerously low, and the medications were not rectifying the issue.

Shortly after this chaos started going on around me, I was informed what had happened and what needed to be done to help me. There were forms I was asked to sign for the procedure. I laughed and said, "I have done this a hundred times." The next thing I remember was being laid flat in the bed and having a cloth draped over my face. Then there it was. A gut-wrenching pain in my neck. I yelled, "Stop, you're hurting me." This chaos around me was scaring the hell out of me. I do remember asking for my phone, and I wanted to speak to Chris. Finally, the call was made to him, and I remembered telling him to come because they did something to me, and I was dying. Bring the kids! Then complete darkness.

What had just happened? I was completely unaware. When I awoke from another eight-hour surgery, my mind and my body were different. The breathing tube was still in, and my body was completely still. I could feel some pain, though. Was I paralyzed? I couldn't move. The questions I needed answered were many. That's when I came into focus and noticed all the doctors and Chris were around me. These surgeons and doctors, I had no clue who they were. The looks on their faces were ones of worry. What did they do to me?

My mind was racing, and I was not ready to hear what happened. Chris, a doctor I had never met, and my Urology surgeon were next to my bed, and the explanation started to come at me. First came the apology for what was done to me. I was told my subclavian artery had been punctured three times by the doctor trying to place a jugular line. After bleeding internally for over forty-two minutes, an X-ray was ordered, and what it showed was emergent. A vascular surgeon was called, and he placed a chest tube to drain the blood pooling in my chest. The internal bleeding had crushed my lungs, and I had to have my chest cracked open to repair the punctures. These puncture wounds were eventually found and patched with a bovine patch. (footnote) My chest was closed and wired back shut. How could this have happened to me? Wasn't I just told the cancer surgery was a success? I was having a hard time comprehending all this news. I was still under some strong anesthesia, and nothing was clear to me. Was I just dreaming this? Then the pain floored me. This was really happening!

How and why? The breathing tube was soon removed. My next-door neighbor was a respiratory technician, and she was visiting and got permission to remove the tube. All I wanted to do was tell her what I remembered. She told me not to talk. I just had to get it out before I lost my memory or my life.

My ability to move slowly returned after a few days. Breathing was very difficult and extremely painful. The full-body pains were unreal. My chest, neck, and abdomen got the worst of it. Which hurts worse, though? My body was now three times bigger than it originally was. I was forty-two pounds heavier. This is when the thoughts overcame me. I started hoping I would just die. It was even a mystery to the doctors how I survived this. The depression was becoming overwhelming! Why did I survive this?

I remember telling Chris that we had to get them for what they did to me, and what this did to you and the kids. The hospital stay lasted for two weeks. Days of no sleep or eating. Tubes were coming out of me everywhere. Breathing hurt, and moving was extremely difficult. I was given a heart-shaped pillow that was supposed to be my assist when trying to get up. I needed to hug that pillow for every movement, including yawning, coughing, or the worst sneezing. There was a note on the board in front of my bed that said I had to get up several times a day and walk. My little leg was gigantic, and it was impossible to put my prosthetic leg on. That note on the board really affected me. Chris had a talk with my surgeon and said it was impossible to do with all the water weight. How was I going to be able to do this? Am I always going to be like this? Will I be able to survive any longer? I couldn't control these thoughts.

Progress was starting to happen to me. I started getting up with help from the medics on the ward. I was finally wheeled down to a giant shower. That was when I realized my back was covered in big, popped blisters from the tape used to hold several drains in place. The water hitting them stung very badly. Every day, I discovered other things that were wrong with me. One day, Chris showed me all my new scars. This deepened my depression. I asked myself daily if I could do this. Chris noticed this in me and tried to make me feel better by putting on some comedians to listen to. It helped, but laughing and smiling were painful. Chris and the kids were my driving force. If I was struggling to do this for myself, I would find it in me to do it for them.

My hospitalization was filled with so many visitors. There were several high-ranking officers, including my husband's boss. I felt like royalty when he visited, and the care I got after his visit was top-class. Some of the wives, family, and local friends also came to check on me and visit. Each visitor was harder to receive than the one prior. I wasn't myself, especially mentally.

It was finally time for me to get discharged. The doctors all agreed I would recover better at home. It would also be more comfortable for me, and I would be able to get some sleep. So, I was on my way home. Getting in and out of the car was a hard endeavor for me. I managed with Chris's help, of course. The only thing I wanted was to lie down in my comfortable bed and finally get some good sleep.

As my recovery was moving along, the thoughts of making them pay for what was done to me became our number one thought. Several lawyers were contacted, and we finally found the one we wanted to handle my case. His passion for getting justice was what I needed in my life at that time. Thinking this would be a positive in my life was quickly smashed. I was still having issues with the memory of how it all happened. There were plenty of weird memories that I had. I was even questioning them. The one that I vividly remembered was being asked to sign a second consent form after I was hurt. I remembered saying I couldn't see the words or the line to sign on. This was when someone said all we need is an X. The pen was placed in my hand and placed on the paper. I did remember just swatting the paper. This paper was never found in my record, but I remember it happening so clearly. I remembered hearing the doctor say she had never done one before. Meaning place the line. But I also remembered a young Asian boy coming in. That one was weird!

During our first meeting with the lawyer, I recalled these memories, but there was no record of any of them. So, we were doing this. We were going to try to sue the Government. Bring it on!

Before we started bringing it on, I was going stir crazy. I needed to get out and be in my happy place, the water. I booked a family whale watching catamaran trip. This outing was a combination of birthdays, anniversaries, and Valentine's Day. I was so excited to be out. Tyler and his girlfriend at the time, Kari, Chris, and I left one Saturday morning. The weather was a little choppy, and so was the sea. We drove out to the North Shore, and the decision was made that we would risk going out. We saw many whales and were heading back in for the day. But that soon changed. Our boat was hit by a forty-foot rogue wave. Several people went overboard. I was the only one left on the front of the boat, and I slid across the front of it. I wrapped my arm around the railing and went into the water. Chris had also reached across the boat and got a hold of my tank top. Our engine blew, and the sail mast broke. All cell phones were wet, and the radio was not working; getting out our Mayday call wasn't happening. We were eventually brought back to shore on jet skis, and I was the only one brought to the hospital. I suffered bruised ribs and a dislocated shoulder. It had only been six months since being injured at the hospital. This was definitely a divine intervention. I survived again, this time a horrible accident. How can these things keep happening to me? I ask myself this repeatedly and always come up with the same answer because I can take it.

Chapter 14: Will This Ever End?

Let the lawsuit, along with all my new health issues, begin. Shortly after "the incident," the name I had given to my life-threatening injury, I started having some serious kidney issues. I attended many medical appointments. New medical specialties, along with the ones I had always been going to for my diabetes care. I was now seeing Urology, Nephrology, and Vascular Surgery monthly. I was getting regular ultrasounds of my chest to check for any fluid in my lungs, my neck, my chest, and my kidneys. This was for checking for fluid in my damaged lungs, checking my subclavian artery for any changes with the patches, and checking for cancer return or any further damage to my kidneys. This has become my full-time job.

My mental state had taken a big hit. I was struggling with getting past the fact that someone else did this to me. Not my diabetes. Not something I did to myself. I was in the hospital to have cancer removed from my left kidney. That surgery went amazingly well, and I was not looking at any long-term health issues. I was going to be released the next day. The day after, I had most of my kidney removed. I know I'm repeating this, but that shows how much of an effect it had on my life.

Time for the lawsuit to get started. This is when I heard all the details of what happened that night. All the injustices. The negligence and malpractice that occurred floored me. After hearing these details, my mental struggles deepened. I started showing signs of severe depression and PTSD. We were reliving this incident daily. It was up to us to get all the medical records from every doctor or hospital I had ever been to. I had to have biopsies of my kidneys performed. There were depositions that had to be made by both parties. I was visited by both an Endocrinologist and a Psychiatrist, who were provided by the government, with questions about my past health issues. Test to see if I was truly suffering from depression and PTSD. I tested very high on both tests. The Government was trying to have its defense concentrate on my diabetes. Their point was that all this was on me and my health.

Not long after these depositions, tests, and questions, the Government admitted to complete negligence and wanted to settle for a very low amount. In the meantime, I was quietly suffering. My kidneys were now in stage four kidney disease, and this was what our lawyers decided was going to be our fighting point. What wasn't fought for was the damage to the rest of my body. I started experiencing severe low blood pressure, which was later diagnosed as autonomic neuropathy. My low blood sugars were going low more often, and I had lost much of my body strength and ability to function on my own. My anxiety and fear got hold of me. Going back to the hospital, the one where I got injured, was the most difficult for me. Too many bad thoughts about that place.

We experienced several delays with our lawsuit, making this even harder for the family and me. It felt much like "Groundhog Day." Tyler started self-medicating, and he was later diagnosed with Schizophrenia. Chris was beginning to show signs of PTSD from his war tours. Kari never talked about what had happened, so it was a mystery as to how she felt. She did have a hard time with her brother, though. THEN THERE WAS ME. I put all my concentration on them. I couldn't see them suffer.

We worked with several doctors to help with Tyler. This was so hard for all of us. This was not his fault! This helped us understand his drug use. These were such confusing times. Chris got the help he needed to learn how to care for himself with PTSD, as always, I put myself last. I did not get proper help in dealing with all my mental turmoil. I put all of myself into getting the lawsuit over, taking care of my kidney disease, and taking care of the family. I dealt with my kidneys going into renal failure twice. I was looking at having to start with dialysis. Luckily, that has never come about. Next came getting put on a transplant list. This was now getting into some serious stuff I'd be dealing with from now on.

Would this lawsuit ever end? Year five now. We finally had to fly back to Hawaii for the court hearing: no jury, only the judge, the lawyers, and us. Tyler was not part of the case because his mental health was not in a good state. During the trial, I learned that my labs were those of a person in the process of dying, a bitter pill to swallow. Kari got a chance to take the stand, and she told her side of the story, bringing all in the courtroom to tears. She later told me that she had never cried about what happened until that day. The judge ruled in our favor, and it was a settlement for much more than the original settlement amount. Of course, the Government appealed and was given another year to rewrite its case. This went down to the last minute, and they finally settled on an amount we accepted. It's finally over! Not really, my new way of life had already started, and I was getting worse. I hate to feel this way, but no amount of money or decision in my favor will ever give me back what I have lost. Could I find another triumph this time? I will, though. That's just who I am!

Chapter 15: The New Me

My life now includes a husband with his struggles, a schizophrenic son with his struggles, a daughter who has been dealing with all these struggles in silence, and me with all my new struggles. I was trying my hardest to deal with everyone else's struggles while not dealing with my own. I needed to turn that switch on myself. But how?

Chris was now retired after thirty years of active duty in the Navy. I had never been so ready for something new, ever. I needed a change. I was in a rut for too long. We had always said we would retire and settle down back in Virginia Beach. We returned to the city we love. This would be the kids' second time living in Virginia Beach, near Grandma and Grandpa. This was a change we were all ready for. Kari had been looking at properties online for months prior to our move, and she found the most wonderful home for us. She took charge, contacted our realtor, and set up a date for us to visit this and several other homes. Nothing appealed to either of us. We just hadn't walked into a house and felt that "This is the one" feeling. Then, in an area I always used to say I would eventually end up living someday, was that house. We loved it, and I immediately saw the potential in this home. My mind went into overdrive. I was now fifty-six, sixteen years past that forty-year mark, and I felt so alive. Not bad!

Chris was now retired from the Navy but found a job at the original hospital where he had worked when we met.

While Chris was working, I was making regular trips to this hospital. Portsmouth, Naval Hospital. Tyler had many appointments with psychiatrists and therapists here as well. I was seeing my regular specialists and several new ones. I was soon referred to an Ear, Nose, and Throat specialist, an ENT. I needed to have a biopsy done on my thyroid. There were several nodules found, which looked very suspicious. I also developed a goiter. What an ugly throat lump! I was scheduled for a lumpectomy, a partial removal of the affected left thyroid. There were early signs of thyroid cancer, so I again dodged another bullet. Easy same-day surgery with no long-term effects on my thyroid function, and the goiter is gone. Praise God!!

The lawsuit was still ongoing, so Chris went back to work until a settlement was reached. Tyler was enrolled in HVAC (tech school) for Heating, Ventilation, and Air Conditioning. Kari was a high school freshman. Chris was able to fully retire with our win against the Government. We have two dogs now, too. Things were moving along at a very fast pace for all of us. This was when Tyler started behaving very oddly. He was caught up in the drugs again. I felt he was self-medicating, and he became so confused. I concentrated on my son and researched dual diagnosis centers. We sent him to California to attend a long-stay dual diagnosis center that would provide the treatment he needed so badly. He was in bad shape, and he needed help with taking care of his mental health. This had a heavy negative effect on all of us. Life was getting extremely difficult for me, and I was not happy with where I was heading with my health and my life. During this time, COVID hit the United

States and shut us down. Both kids had to finish school at home. Kari started homeschooling in her senior year, and Tyler finished his schoolwork online. We learned to deal with it, but it was making matters worse in our home.

We had become financially fit, and one would think all would be wonderful, but I was ready for something new. I suggested we sponsor an exchange student. We sponsored a young lady from Spain. She stayed with us for her entire Junior year of high school. We traveled to California to visit Tyler, New York, to see Hamilton, and we regularly went to Corolla, North Carolina. We experienced some amazing things during her stay, and she was happy. She was the top tennis player for high school, receiving the MVP award. Such a strong young lady to leave her family and her country for a year. This was a big distraction, especially for Tyler and me, and our health issues. Then my hardships returned, even for her, during this time with us. She struggled with COVID at the same time as Kari. Poor girls. Chris and I stayed COVID free during this time. While she was still with us, I dealt with some things that she experienced along with the family. I took a nasty fall one evening in the winter. Landed on our deck. I tripped over the dogs while taking them out to use the bathroom. My pelvis was fractured in two places. I had fractured my hip years before, so I knew what I was in for. Recovery would be long and very difficult. I felt for the girls. But they stepped up and helped me immensely. It was difficult for them to see me struggle with even moving the slightest. The tears and yelling were a lot for them to witness. This left a mark on them, and Chris didn't like seeing me back in this situation. I didn't want to be their burden, but they saw me trying to do a lot on my own, and they weren't having it. It was a month later, and I remembered the girls taking me out to see the Christmas lights that I loved seeing every holiday. I was starting to feel like I was back, but was I? I now have a constant ache in my right pelvis. But I can still walk. My limp is now a little more pronounced, and it's more painful to deal with, but I made the best of it. I was sad to see the girls have to deal with this, but I prayed they saw my strength in my recovery, and it will stay with them always.

The year was now getting back on track for us. This is when my mother, the kids called her GMA, became extremely ill and passed away shortly after. Our exchange student was still living with us during this time. That was good for Kari to have her here during this time. My mom and Kari had a close, loving relationship. Kari was having a hard time dealing with this loss. I miss my mom so much! The time our student spent with our family gave her a real look at what life throws your way. She saw how we, especially me, handled these life moments to bounce back better and stronger because of them. This stay must have made quite the impression on our exchange student. She recently informed me she may return to the US to do another exchange program, only this time as a college senior.

Life in the household was different. There was still unconditional love between us, but it felt entirely different to me. Tyler was gone and had some major psychotic breaks. Kari graduated from high school and wanted to go away to college. Chris was doing his own thing. My independence has suffered over the last few years. Getting around has become extremely difficult for me. My anxiety was worsening, even when I left the house. I became fearful of driving anywhere on my own. The question, "Can I do this on my own?" became a regular question for me. The questions every time we ventured out were: Do we need to bring the wheelchair? Can I make it through the trip? Am I going to get ill from my diabetes or my kidneys? So many things were thrown into a simple trip outside the house. Traveling on my own is now something I can't enjoy. I used to love traveling on my own. There isn't too much I do on my own anymore. My night vision has gotten much worse, even worse than it was early in my life. So, going out at night is another set of questions that need answers before we leave. Even seeing 3-D has become difficult for me when it gets darker. I can't judge the curbs. I always need assistance from whoever is with me to help me up or down the curbs. I have, in my broken eyes, become a burden to others. The family has told me that I am not a burden in any way, but my mental state does not let me accept this. Losing my independence has left a lasting mark on my life.

Appointments are my main life events now. There are transplant workups I must attend yearly. A day full of seeing different specialists, with even needing my husband to attend some of these with me, especially the ones that are in the city. My kidney function has declined immensely. I suffer from regular kidney infections and now kidney stones. Dealing with these issues has become routine for me. I try my hardest to look past these many issues and try my hardest to enjoy what life I still have.

I still try to have some adventurous times, and I love to experience new things. I did IFLY, indoor skydiving, spent a lot of time going down to the beach house, and even took a trip to Alaska with some of my family for a fishing expedition. I am so into seeing wildlife and its natural beauty. Recently, we went on a nine-day cruise back there to Alaska with my best friend and Chris. This trip was a total sightseeing trip and our first cruise. I see more of these cruises in my future.

Despite these good days, I still have my everyday struggles and some major hardships, including being hospitalized twice. First was a severe pain I was experiencing in my abdomen. After several hours in the Emergency room, I was brought to the surgery ward after the discovery of a large kidney stone. This was the first one I have ever experienced at that level. I had a stent placed and ended up spending a week in the hospital. My triumph was that my diabetes stayed in control. Several weeks later, the day before Thanksgiving, I returned to have the stone blasted and the stent removed. That surgery went well, although I suffered from some PTSD. The nurses and two doctors had a very difficult time placing my IV lines. Reminiscent of the incident. All was fine, and my recovery was quick. Stone in the past. Triumph!

On Christmas Day, I started running a high temperature. I became very nauseous and started throwing up. My fever was so high that I could not even stand on my own. Chris called the paramedics, and I was taken to the hospital again. This time, I had bilateral kidney infections, and I had sepsis. There was an infection running wild within my system, and I feared that I would start losing organ function. This was a rough stay. I was having issues with my blood pressure, my heart rhythm, and some high blood sugars, and I had to take more medicines. The new medications were cleaning out the infection, and I started feeling stir crazy in the hospital. We all truly thought the worst was behind us, but no, the big kicker with this stay was yet to come. Kari and I had our wallets stolen from my hospital room. Thousands of dollars were spent on my cards before we even realized they were gone. It was my idea for Chris and Kari to come visit and bring my Scrabble board for something different. I just wanted to leave my room for a few minutes and play some Scrabble. That mess was taken care of, and I recovered fine, and I was feeling back to what I have felt was my normal for years now. Not the strongest, but anything was better than what I had just gone through. Another struggle that has come out as a triumph.

It was now early February 2025. I had been putting off having a complete shoulder replacement of my right shoulder for long enough. I was off all antibiotics, and there were no longer any infections present in my system. I had made a full recovery from the kidney issues. Time to tackle this shoulder issue. Luckily, this surgery was a same-day procedure. So, no overnight stays for me. But that is if all goes well. The surgery was completed, I had a new shoulder, and I didn't have to stay overnight. The recovery period is long and full of daily physical therapy. I was getting the chance to leave the house for several days a week. This lasted for six months. I was ahead of schedule for the rehab, and the pain is almost completely unnoticeable. My scar is already barely noticeable as well. I have close to full use of this shoulder back. I am now nearing thirty surgeries in my sixty years of life. Still finding the triumphs with every surgery. Maybe I should consider having the left shoulder done as well, maybe in the near future.

Chapter 16: Head Games

I've been getting through all the physical traumas I have faced throughout my life, thinking I was being triumphant. Maybe I was getting past the physical aspect of these traumas, but how was I doing mentally? Never faced the psychological toll these traumas have taken on me. I needed to stop hiding the fact that I was truly suffering emotionally. I played the role of the strong one, but I truly despised that word "strong." I found it hard to admit that at times I was weak. It's just not how others saw me. Can I keep this fakeness up?

I found every excuse I could to write it off. I was going through menopause at this time as well, so that's what it had to be, right? I had been tested, observed, and later told by the defense's psychiatrist that I was suffering from PTSD, and the test also revealed I was severely depressed after what I had been through with the incident. It was hard for me to accept. I could not show people this side of me. I had a son diagnosed with schizophrenia and a husband suffering from post-war PTSD. My daughter suffered from clinical depression that was newly diagnosed. I had to remain strong. I stepped aside, and I recommended that Chris get some intense outpatient care for himself, and we made sure Tyler was getting taken care of with his disease. I also made sure my daughter got into therapy and took care of her depression. I made sure that what needed to be done for them became my priority. But what about me? I told myself I could handle what I was going through.

It was never really anything I thought about. Just make sure they are all getting what they need to stay healthy.

It was suggested to me repeatedly that I seek some intense therapy of my own. The only concern for me was, on top of all the follow-up appointments, the physical therapy, and my regular specialists, when would I find the time to add this? Well, that time never came for me. I kept trying to convince myself and everyone else that I was ok. Time kept moving on. I started feeling like I was dying inside and I was losing my happiness. I did try my hardest to hide it. It wasn't until I let this new me almost destroy my marriage. I wasn't fooling anyone, including myself anymore. I was broken and I needed to get myself back. I needed to fix myself. I knew who I still was deep down, and I was miserable being this new person that I had become. I didn't recognize this person, it wasn't me. Enough was enough! Finding my happiness is now the only way for me to go. Everyone else is fine and is able to take care of themselves. It's my time now!

I got myself the therapy that I truly needed. I was ready to take this therapy seriously. No more faking it. I started to realize that despite all my traumas and the many scars that go along with those traumas, I am beautiful, and I am a great person. People see me for me and not all my traumas. I need to love myself again, and I deserve more credit than I ever give myself. I am now doing things I always thought were corny, like reading my daily affirmations. I have a list of them taped to my dresser mirror, so there's no missing them. I write in my journal from time to time, and I wrote this book. This book has let me let go and not dwell on the things

I've been through and am still going through. That doesn't define me. I now believe in that word, the word used to describe me by so many others, STRONG! That's a powerful word to me now. I am alright with being weak at times. That's just human nature, and I'm not above it. I am getting better at accepting compliments like I never had before. I'm finding my happiness again, and it feels good, and I did it on my own! It feels great to be happy!

Going back to church was another thing on my list to do. My daughter introduced me to a pastor and others at her church. I found the sermons hitting me so profoundly. I felt like Kari and I were the only ones there in the church, and we were being talked to directly. It was a profound feeling. This helped me stop questioning God and start believing there is a reason for everything that happens. There are always lessons to learn.

It is a slow process, but in time, I will be the person I used to be once again. That adventurous person I missed for the last six years. This is all despite my old age. Forty can kiss off. I'm sixty now and waiting for my next adventures to take shape. My list is starting to become long. There are still so many things I would like to do before it's too late.

Chapter 17: Losing Mom

2022 April. My mother had been deteriorating with her health for several years now. She had suffered a couple of heart incidents and became more and more immobile. I got a call one morning from my father saying your mother is in the hospital and I need to get there at once. She was in the Intensive Care Unit, and it wasn't looking good for her. She had suffered a stroke and had several abscesses in her intestines. She went into surgery after the doctors discovered these issues, and drains were placed to clear the infection from these abscesses. While she was there, she had atrial fibrillation, A-fib, and her heart rate got up into the 140 range. We didn't know what was causing this, but she was showing symptoms almost like Alzheimer's. She wasn't sure who we were. Even my dad. We think it was because of the stroke and the severity of her condition.

We were all scared for her. She was eighty years old at this time. Walking was no longer something she could do. Her legs and ankles were all turned in, and she couldn't work with the physical therapists. She would complain that her legs were hurting too much to get up on them. Every time they came in to get her up, her heart would speed up, and she would go into A-fib. This was scary for the therapy team, and they would return her to the room and then leave. My brother had come in from California by now to help with whatever he could. My father was happy to have him around during this time. He was able to tackle some projects around the house, which were exactly what my dad needed. It was so hard to see her like this.

She stayed in the hospital for two weeks, and now my sister was there as well to help with her care. After the hospital, she spent some more time in a rehab hospital, and because of her lack of progress, she was released to spend what the nursing staff knew were her final days.

My sister was her caregiver while she was back at home. We turned the dining room into a hospital room for her. She was never able to get out of that bed again. Thank God for my sister's unselfishness in coming and doing this for our father. My gratitude to her is immeasurable.

Mom lived for a week after getting home. She got all her senses back and loved for us to sit and talk with her. She told stories of her younger life. It was so amazing that she still had so many memories that she remembered so vividly. We tried to keep her spirit up, and my sister kept her smiling and laughing.

The night prior to her death, she had what I learned was called "terminal lucidity." She told my sister she wanted to do some of her PT and was feeling great. It was wonderful to hear her say this. There were still those little bits of hope. My sister found her the next morning.

I know she is watching over all of us, especially our father. I feel her presence every day. It's still hard realizing she's gone. I find myself seeing or hearing something and thinking to myself, I can't wait to tell Mom about this one. There are times my father will do something, and my sister and I think the same thing.

Mom would get a kick out of this one. I saved a message from her on voicemail and listened to it from time to time to hear her voice again, and to actually laugh at the message she was sending.

We miss you, Mom! Rest in peace...

Chapter 18: A Family Progress Report

Chris and I, and our relationship, had taken a big hit during these times. Even got close to a divorce and even him thinking he could find companionship elsewhere. This was a rude awakening for us both, mostly for me. I finally realized I needed to get some real help. It was my time to take care of my mental health. It was my time, for me! With all these triumphs after the hardships in my life, I just couldn't get my mental health right. I had to do better for myself. First was to find and start with an amazing therapist, and start caring for and about myself as I cared about and for everyone else. I did just that, and I am happy I did. With her help and words of encouragement, I spoke with my husband and suggested we go to a marriage retreat in Sedona, Arizona. It was what we needed. I felt he needed to hear what I am going through with my trauma and this new life I now live. Also, my mental health struggles. I needed to hear how I was neglecting our marriage and him. It all got brought out during this retreat and made us both stop and listen to each other, a great learning experience for us both.

The retreat was a big success. No lie, it was a bit corny for me, but we reconnected and renewed our truth in our love for one another. Another triumph in our lives.

My son is now in California after completing his year-long program and has been there for over five years. He is now a homeowner and is dealing with all that goes along with owning your own home. We still help in any way we can. There have been other endeavors my son has ventured into, but his true love is computers and everything that goes with them. He attended several coding classes online, and I hope this is what he finds happiness in.

My beautiful daughter found her calling during this time, as well. She tried going to college out of state and was not successful with that endeavor. She missed her mom and the closeness we shared. All the college drama was a bit much for her, so she returned home, tried the local community college again, but just wasn't happy with this path either. She was taking notice of me and all the health issues I dealt with. That's when she made the most life-altering decision she would ever make. She wanted to be a nurse. Something I would never have thought she would be interested in. She fooled us all. She is attending an accelerated nursing program and feels happy about this path. She found her calling, a triumph for my baby girl. I'll always see both kids as my babies. That will never change.

Our family has a way of honoring one another. We do this through tattoos. Chris and I got our first tattoos in Hawaii. I have my favorite flower, the hibiscus, and in the banner, I added Chris's name, and in the leaves, I put the kids' initials. Chris did the same with my name on the banner and the kids' initials on his military rank tattoo. Tyler was next to get a tattoo. He had put on his wrist and hand a beautiful flower. He told me he got this because of me. When Kari turned seventeen, she wanted a tattoo. She wanted to get two butterflies on her inside wrist. She wanted me to get the same exact one. I did, and we now have our mother-daughter symbol on our inner arm. My next tattoo was put on my right back shoulder. It's two hearts with the kids' names written as part of the lines of the heart. I will get one more. This one is going to be on my right arm, and this will be a barbed wire heart to represent Tyler, one of his favorite tattoos. I am done now, no more tattoos for me.

My love for my family is so deep, unconditional, and will always be this way. My family is what it is, but it works for us, as strange as that may sound. The struggles will always be present in our lives, but dealing with and triumphing over them is what we have learned to do together on our journey. Yes, there will be more lessons to learn and more medical hardships for me, but this is my journey, our journey, and we will always be learning and triumphing together until the end.

Today, my day ended how I always imagined. I spent the day with Kari and had the most wonderful conversation with Tyler. I felt the love, and I was truly happy. Those love bombs are therapy for me.

Chapter 19: My Biggest Gifts

"Not flesh of my flesh nor bone of my bone, but still miraculously my own. Never forget for a single minute you didn't grow under my heart, but in it!"

Children bring us joy and pain. Most of all, they show unconditional love. I have always experienced this with my two beautiful children. They have no problem showing me and telling me how much they love me and how proud they are to have me as their mom. I return their unconditional love, and I beam with pride. That's a given! They have grown to be beautiful adults and will someday create a lovely family of their own. Fingers crossed, they give Chris and me some grandkids.

We have all been on this rollercoaster of a life together and have weathered more than any family should. God chose us, though. We all accepted this ride, got on board, and are riding it together, the good, the bad, the ugly, and the outcomes of it all. We chose not to let this define us.

My children are just as strong as I am. I see this in them every time I look at them. My son is showing his strength daily with his condition, at times not even realizing how strong he is in dealing with it. Even though it is tough for others to see it, I know that strength in him every day. His life is a difficult one. Not knowing how his mind will work from day to day. He is paranoid that people are out to hurt him, so sometimes he doesn't see that most, especially me and the family, only want to help him in any way we can. I've learned to talk calmly with him and stop and listen. I know he feels my love down deep. He has saved me several times, and I can't tell him enough how amazed and thankful I am with him. My son, you are strong!

My daughter shows me her strength every day as well. She has taken her experiences with me and is using them for the betterment of others. It makes me happy to be there for her when she needs a caring mother. She assures me all the time that our talks and our mother-daughter days brighten her spirit. The laughs we share together are always flowing. The two of us are very similar in our sense of humor and can find humor in even the most mundane. We also share similar interests, like mother and daughter. Her life path has mimicked mine in so many ways. I have to say that, as much as I try to be there for her, she is always there for me.

It is unimaginable to me the things that they have experienced. They had seen their mother being wheeled down the hall under a blanket with one foot sticking out, all ashen from the loss of blood. Not knowing if they would ever see me again. Just the thought of this brings tears to my eyes. The thing is, they will not remember me that way. They see me as the mom who is fun, adventurous, daring, mostly happy, and loves to laugh. The mother who is always willing to put herself aside for them. I still see them to this day as my little kids. They both have a great sense of humor, are adventurous, and are not afraid to try new things. I would love to think they have taken these characteristics from me.

My children are always first on my mind upon waking up, going to sleep, after receiving bad news, coming out of anesthesia, and even coming out of my low blood sugar comas. First and foremost, wondering how the kids are doing. If they are ok, can they handle another one of my medical hardships? They have seen the worst of me. The amputation and the coma my son experienced right by my side. The news that the two of them got from me was that I had cancer. Worst of all was the 2014 incident. They always managed to hide from me their true feelings about how they experience all this and how it has mentally taken its toll on them. Always staying positive on my behalf. I know that deep down, they live with the fear of losing me. I try my hardest to reassure them I'm not planning on ever stopping my fight, and I will never quit. I am the woman who wouldn't quit.

We are all blessed with our faith and have seen God do his work over and over. Our family may call on him a little more than most. We have no idea what is in store for us next. I thank God daily for the family he has brought me. I will continue being there for my children. I will be their companion, therapist, and advisor. But, most of all, I will be their mother! I feel I have found my purpose!

Chapter 20: The Gift of Life

The medical hardships I have endured have been many. But the triumphs that came from these struggles have made me who I am to this day. Struggles should not define you, but they should make you stronger. Finding your strength will become your asset. I am proof of this.

The scars will always be there, but I now see these scars as reminders of what I have been through. I wear them like my tattoos. I wear them with pride. It is not rare for me to get those pity looks and awe from other people after hearing just a part of my story. They see the many scars all over my body and my prosthetic leg, but after these people get to know me, they see my strength and endurance and my sense of humor, which I thankfully still have; they become somewhat amazed that I am that same person they have heard many stories about. Well, I am that person, and I'm able to own up to it.

It is hard for me to hear others say that they could never go through what I have been through. That's not true! If anyone were in my shoes, they would find their inner strength and triumph over all their struggles. Struggles are normal. Getting through those struggles is what makes you, YOU!

Prayer is a big part of my life as well. I pray to God for him to put on me what my family members are struggling with. I am strong, and I can handle anything. I have shown that repeatedly. I don't want to see anyone else suffer. Give it to me and spare them.

I was having a little trouble with how to end this book the right way. It was suggested to me by my Physical Therapist to have others write it for me. I've decided to do just that. I have asked several people who truly matter to me and have gone through a lot of these struggles right by my side. You are going to read a few lines from them all on how they see me. I hope their words will give you the true picture of me and my strength. I truly love each and every one of them and appreciate all they have done for me. Their encouragement and their ability to make me feel needed and wanted!

Here are their words, from the people who know me best. The people I owe my life to. The people who are my biggest advocates. The people I owe my deepest thank you. I mean this from the bottom of my heart. I love you all!

Daughter Kari, My Baby Girl.

When people think of their mom, it can be good, bad, happy, and sad. But when I think of my mom, I think of my best friend. From the start, my mom has been my rock. She has always gone above and beyond for everyone in her life, especially my brother and me. From planning extravagant birthdays to creating special moments for every holiday, she makes life almost as special as she is. I could go on and on about how strong my mom is and all the battles she has overcome, but to me, she's so much more than that. My mom is someone who has turned every bad day into a good day. Every stressful situation, into a positive solution. I mean it when I say that she's meant to be a mother. I hope to be even half as amazing a mother to my future children. We all know she's going to be the favorite grandma. It's so hard to truly express how much I love my mom! She has saved my life in dark times, and I don't think I'd be the woman I am today if it weren't for her. She's just as beautiful on the inside as she is on the outside. I hope she never changes who she is because Mom, you are enough! My mom is one for putting everyone first before herself. Mom, it's your turn now....

Son Tyler, My heart.

Mom, I appreciate all you do for me, Thank You so much, and I love you!!!

Father, Man of few words.

Paula's story about her life is an extraordinary story. She is one of a kind and will continue to be an extraordinary daughter, wife and mother.

Sister Jennifer, The funny one, and my bestie.

After every medical crisis, you bounce back. AND DO IT SOBER! We don't know how you do it. You just do it. My favorite quote "To succeed in life you need a wishbone, a backbone, and a funny bone." That's all you Sister.

Sister Denise, also a cancer survivor.

'You have two options when all is stacked against you medically and emotionally. Give up or fight like Hell' Lance Armstrong. Paula, you are a fighter and a survivor! Paula has suffered from type 1 diabetes, Kidney and thyroid cancer, and a botched medical procedure that almost took her life. My little sister has lived through more personal challenges than any other person I know and has come through them to inspire me and everyone who knows her. Keep on fighting Paula!

Brother Doug. My overseer.

The beginning of her fight. I don't think I'll ever forget the first time I saw Paula so sick, so fragile. We were kids then, but I knew, even in that moment, something had changed. Something serious. I can still remember her lying pale and weak there. At that moment, I felt a surge of hopelessness. I hadn't known before. I was supposed to protect her, to be the strong one for her. Here she was, vulnerable, in a way I couldn't fix. No number of words of encouragement could change what was happening. I couldn't fight for her.

We had no idea how hard her journey would be. How many more days in hospitals? How many more times I would hold her hand when she felt too weak to stand on her own. I did know one thing. Paula was strong. Stronger than I could ever be, and no matter what would come next, I would stand by her side.... Because I know she will never stop fighting.

Brother Greg. The oldest of us all.

Paula has a unique level of psychological resilience that has allowed her to overcome countless crises throughout her life. She is admired by me, family, and friends alike for her ability to overcome life's challenges and recover without evident setbacks. I encourage her to share her life's story of how she has dealt with the mental and physical difficulties of living with chronic diabetes. She was first diagnosed at a young age of twelve and has endured losing her right leg below the knee and the deterioration of her eyesight. I admire her character and her vitality, and that's what makes her so special!

Sister Lynda, the youngest, and the family's Hawaiian surprise.

They say a cat has nine lives. For a person not fond of felines, Paula has a lot in common with them. How many times can you outsmart the Grim Reaper? Quite a few, actually. I grew up seeing Paula sick a lot. I remember my mom asking me how I always woke up when Paula had insulin reactions in the night. Several nights, waking my parents up to help her. We had a special bond. I had a sixth sense as a kid. Still do. Her whole life has been in and out of hospitals. We bonded over her sugar-free Jello. I was always afraid. To this day, I gag at the smell of hospitals. And if you have ever been in a military hospital, trust me on that one. Never sure if she was going to make it was a different and new issue but always equally terrifying.

Fast forward to us being grown-ups. She has been through so much. Each phone call from our mom was another "they are not sure she will make it out." My sister Jennifer and I went to Dallas on one of those occasions. Paula was in a coma. Her very young son had called 911. We heard the recording of it. He was scared, confused but so very, very brave. He just wanted his mom to be ok. We visited the hospital. She was on breathing machines, and they were talking to Chris about hospice care because her brain was not responding. I just remember looking at the slope of the sheets. I had not seen her since her amputation. I wanted to look so bad. You guessed it, I did. Then Jennifer being Jennifer said something stupid, and we started to crack up. I saw Paula move. She tried to laugh. I told her if she didn't wake up Jennifer was going to stay forever and make her life a living hell. She squeezed my hand. Once again... She's alive! How many times has she made it out of the woods? Lost count. Don't be surprised if she just had surgery to remove her Thyroid because of cancer but managed to tile her fireplace the day after getting out of the hospital. That is how she rolls. And the leg? Who needs two? Gotta have a sense of humor about it. The looks she gets from them are incredible. Whether throwing her swim leg with the painted plastic toenails in the pool at our parents' 50th anniversary for the grandkids to float on or taking it off and on the beach while we were swimming with white tip sharks. Absolutely scared the shit out of those tourists. Worth it.

She is a trooper. She is not done yet. Not today, Satan. Not today

Best Friend, Cheryl, another cancer survivor buddy.

Paula is a dear friend who taught me the courage it takes to face the challenges that come as we journey through life. The resilience to make it through to the other side while always keeping the humor in the moment, and the strength to live life fully. Through each challenge, she rose above and survived.

May her book give hope to those facing obstacles in their lives and healing.

One of our friend group, Tina

Paula is my Shero!

Another friend of our group, Jennifer

You are a woman warrior and a survivor. Whenever you get knocked down, you always get back up. You're strong, brave, resilient, and unstoppable.

You stay positive in the face of adversity. You personify the saying "That which does not kill us, makes us stronger." You are an inspiration.

Another friend of our group, Belinda

Paula, you are one of the strongest women I know, a true warrior..." She made broken look beautiful and strong look invincible. She walked with the universe on her shoulders and made it look like a pair of wings."— Ariana Dancu.

The last of our friend group, Ginny

I have no idea what to say, but Paula is a very strong and determined woman.

Long-time friend, Alida

Paula owns a piece of my heart. The strength I've seen in her through the years is what makes her a one-of-a-kind, remarkable woman.

Therapist, My saving grace.

Paula is an amazing, brave woman who has faced numerous hardships far beyond what many could fathom, yet she chooses to inspire others and walk with integrity.

I have witnessed firsthand the amount of courage she embodies through the most complicated and harrowing of times. Paula has continued to care for so many others. Her kindness, selflessness, and faith in God have been a light and inspiration to those around her, and she has remained humble, even with a testimony as big as hers.

I believe this book could be an encouragement for those facing some of life's most difficult challenges, both physically and mentally.

Friend Chris.

When I first met Paula, I felt pain for her due to everything that had happened and still was happening due to that horrible accident. But, as the years have gone by, she has left me in awe. Paula doesn't let what she went through define her. She is strong! I know she doesn't like that word, but she is that. She is also funny, caring, intelligent, loving, generous, and a great friend with a huge ear for listening. I am, and I know a lot of people who are grateful to have her a part of their lives. So proud of you!

Afterword

For 34 years, I have had the honor of standing beside the strongest person I have ever known. Paula has faced unimaginable trials and yet continues to rise, time and time again. Since the age of twelve, she has taken on type 1 diabetes, the loss of her right leg, countless surgeries, and near-death experiences, yet she moves forward with a grace and determination that humbles everyone around her. There is no challenge too great, no hardship that can break her spirit.

She endured my deployments and combat tours. She bore the weight of this with strength and unwavering love, keeping our family together. She did this for twenty-eight of the thirty years I served in the United States Navy. We adopted our two children, and when our son was diagnosed with schizophrenia, his battle became hers. She has walked with him through it all; she has remained steadfast, never once wavering in her love or her hope. Beyond all she has endured, she has given our daughter the greatest gift, a shining example of what it means to be a powerful woman. They are bound by love, laughter, and an unbreakable connection. She is one who would fight to the death to protect her children. She teaches by example, showing them how to stand tall in the face of adversity and carry themselves with strength and grace, no matter what storms may come.

What truly defines Paula is not just her endurance but her heart. I have heard her pray, "God, please take away the illnesses and sickness from my friends and family and give them to me." That is the kind of person she is, one who would willingly bear the suffering of others if it meant easing their pain.

If resilience had a face, it would be hers. If grace under pressure had a name, it would be hers. Nothing stops her. Nothing dims her light. She is a warrior in every sense of the word, and I am forever grateful to walk this journey with her. When I prayed to God for strength in my life and in marriage, He sent me Paula. She is the answer to that prayer, a woman whose resilience, love, and unwavering faith have carried us through life's most difficult battles. She is not just my wife; she is my rock, my inspiration, and the greatest blessing I could ever have received. And on top of all that, she is the most beautiful woman in the world!

Christopher Aldis, Navy Command Master Chief (Ret), and above all, Paula's husband

Family Memories

Aldis Wedding Renewal, Marco Island, FL
September 24, 2011

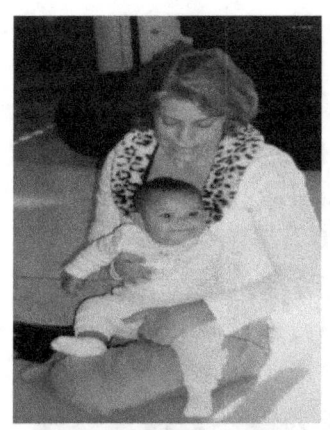

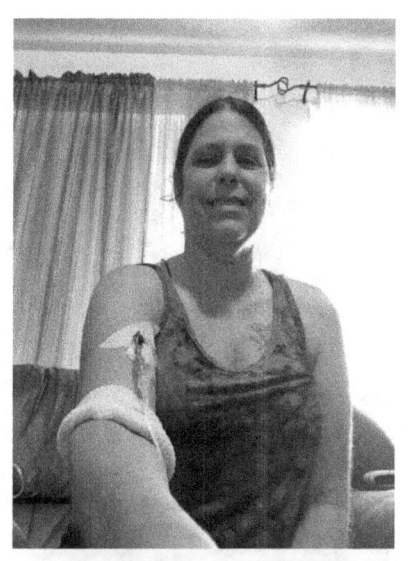

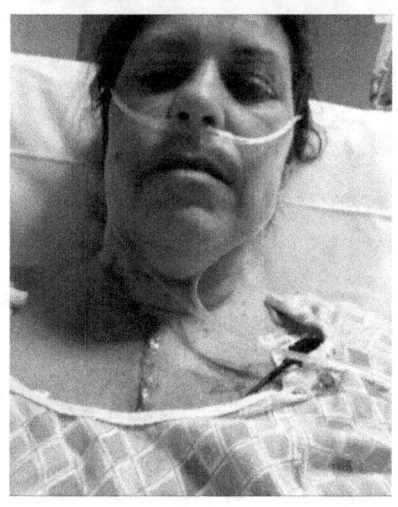